P9-AFZ-334

The American Classics

Also by Denis Donoghue

The Third Voice: Modern British and American Verse Drama

Connoisseurs of Chaos: Ideas of Order in Modern American Poetry

An Honoured Guest: New Essays on W. B. Yeats (editor, with J. R. Mulryne)

The Ordinary Universe: Soundings in Modern Literature

Jonathan Swift: A Critical Introduction

Emily Dickinson

Jonathan Swift: A Critical Anthology (editor)

William Butler Yeats

W. B. Yeats: Memoirs—Autobiography: First Draft (editor)

Thieves of Fire

Seven American Poets (editor)

The Sovereign Ghost: Studies in Imagination

Poems of R. P. Blackmur (editor)

Ferocious Alphabets

The Arts Without Mystery

We Irish: Essays on Irish Literature and Society

Selected Essays of R. P. Blackmur (editor)

Reading America: Essays on American Literature

England, Their England: Commentaries on English Language and Literature

America in Theory (editor, with Louis Menand and Leslie Berlowitz)

Warrenpoint

Being Modern Together

The Pure Good of Theory

The Old Moderns: Essays on Literature and Theory

Walter Pater: Lover of Strange Souls

The Practice of Reading

Words Alone: The Poet T. S. Eliot

Adam's Curse: Reflections on Literature and Religion

Speaking of Beauty

The American Classics

A PERSONAL ESSAY

Denis Donoghue

YALE UNIVERSITY PRESS   NEW HAVEN AND LONDON

Published with assistance from the foundation established in memory of
Philip Hamilton McMillan of the class of 1894, Yale College.

Designed by Rebecca Gibb.
Set in Baskerville type by
Integrated Publishing Solutions.
Printed in the United States of America.

Library of Congress Cataloging-in-Publication Data
Donoghue, Denis.
The American Classics : a personal essay / Denis Donoghue.
p. cm.
Includes bibliographical references and index.
ISBN 0-300-10781-1 (cloth : alk. paper)
1. American literature—19th century—History and criticism—
Theory, etc. 2. Canon (Literature) I. Title.
PS201.D665 2005
810.9′003—dc22
2004023264

A catalogue record for this book is available from the British Library.

The paper in this book meets the guidelines for permanence and durability
of the Committee on Production Guidelines for Book Longevity
of the Council on Library Resources.

10 9 8 7 6 5 4 3 2 1

Again for Frances

Contents

INTRODUCTION

After Emerson

I

I started thinking of writing this book in the autumn of 2003, when I taught a graduate course at New York University called Five in American Literature. The books I chose to teach, if they didn't choose themselves, were *The Scarlet Letter, Moby-Dick, Leaves of Grass, Walden,* and *Huckleberry Finn.* I assumed that these were the American classics and that I didn't need to make a case for reading them; they could be taken for granted, subject to the risk entailed by that status of their not being taken at all. I thought it would be worthwhile to discuss them with a group of graduate students, on the understanding that they had read these books in high school and might welcome an occasion to read them again in a different moral and political setting and with different issues in view. A classic, I was content to think, is a book one reads at least twice. I needed all the information I could get about the presence of these books in American education and culture. I came to the United States in my middle years to take up an appointment at New York University, so I have not attended an American primary or secondary school, college or university. I wanted to discover what it meant that these five books have been accepted by American culture as the cardinal books. What does this acceptance say of the culture? How do American readers use them; in the service of what causes?

It is no offense to the students to report that they did not help me much to answer these questions. It turned out that none of the students had read all the books. Some of them had read one or two of them, but only in excerpts: two or three of the more agreeable chapters of *Walden,* the "Custom-House" introduction to *The Scarlet Letter,* a few anthology poems from *Leaves of Grass.* When I pressed the matter, I was allowed to think that Ayn Rand had a more palpable presence in their high schools than Whitman or Melville. The students did not dispute that the five books are somehow privileged in American culture, but so are the heads on Mount Rushmore; stared at rather than otherwise appreciated. I gathered from the students that the five books had little provenance in their own early education. *To Kill a Mockingbird* meant more to them.

So I couldn't—and can't—answer the questions I posed about the books and their bearing on American culture. I can only read them as they seem to me to ask to be read. To be read now, that is, at a time when "the violence without"—Stevens's phrase—makes it nearly impossible to exert "the violence within," the force of intelligence and imagination, in response to it. Afghanistan, Iraq—and what next?—Israel's Sharon triumphant in Bush's Washington, the Palestinians brushed aside, the American empire enforcing itself commercially and militarily (even though Niall Ferguson claims in *Colossus* that most Americans don't want to be imperial and would prefer to be building more shopping malls)? What is the point of reading books at such a time, when reality is defined as military power, vengeance, "the war on terror," and oil? But what else can one do but read books?

2

I have called these five books classics. The word is often used casually, seldom stringently. Casually, as in referring to a classic detective story, cookbook, or silent film; stringently, when we mark the boundary within which we intend using the word and fend off rival meanings. T. S. Eliot's use of the word is exemplary in this respect. In 1944 he gave the Presidential Address to the Virgil Society under the title "What Is a Classic?" He acknowledged that the word has "several meanings in several contexts," while he claimed to be concerned with "one meaning in one context." He used the word so strictly that, reading the printed lecture for the first time, you would wonder how he could find a single work to answer to his definition. A work is a classic, according to Eliot, only if three conditions are fully met: the manners of the civilization which it articulates must be mature, the language of that civilization must be mature, and the imagination of the particular writer must be mature. Eliot explained at length what he meant by "maturity," mainly by associating the word with cognate words and phrases. Maturity is characterized by a balance between tradition and the individual talent: it depends on the ripeness of a language, "community of taste," and possession of "a common style." A common style "is one which makes us exclaim, not 'this is a man of genius using the language' but 'this realizes the genius of the language.'" The marks of immaturity are provincialism, a limited range of sensibility, and eccentricity. A theory of the impersonality of the work of literature sustains Eliot's idea of the classic and of the maturity that characterizes it: what he fears is the willfulness of a writer who flouts the genius of the language. The three criteria are fulfilled, so far as European literature is in question, only in Virgil's *Aeneid* and Dante's *Divine Comedy*. The critical value of considering these poems as classics is that they provide a criterion, they make us take seriously the question of critical evaluation when other poems and works of literature are in question. Eliot did not propose to consider in that lecture, as he does in "The Dry Salvages," the status of *Bhagavad-Gita* or any other work that may have classic force in cultures beyond Europe. For the time being, he is concerned only with Europe and with a strict designation of a classic in that context. In that sense, English literature does not contain a classic; nor does French. Goethe's poetry is a classic, but not what Eliot calls a *universal* classic:

> We may speak justly enough of the poetry of Goethe as constituting a classic, because of the place which it occupies in its own language and literature. Yet, because of its partiality, of the impermanence of some of its content, and the germanism of the sensibility; because Goethe appears, to a foreign eye, limited by his age, by his language, and by his culture, so that he is unrepresentative of the whole European tradition, and, like our own nineteenth-century authors, a little provincial, we cannot call him a *universal* classic.[1]

This entails a distinction "between the relative and the absolute classic," between a work that, to become what it is, has had to exclude many possibilities of the language in which it is written and a work which has not had to make any such exclusion. The sacrifice of some potentialities of a language in order to realize others, Eliot says, "is a condition of artistic creation, as it is a condition of life, in general." Nonetheless, a certain wholeness is possible in literature:

> We may come to the conclusion, then, that the perfect classic must be one in which the whole genius of a people will be latent, if not all revealed; and that it can only appear in a language such that its whole genius can

> be present at once. We must accordingly add, to our list of characteristics of the classic, that of *comprehensiveness.* The classic must, within its formal limitations, express the maximum possible of the whole range of feeling which represents the character of the people who speak that language. It will represent this at its best, and it will also have the widest appeal: among the people to which it belongs, it will find its response among all classes and conditions of men.[2]

Eliot does not claim—it would be meaningless—that Virgil and Dante are the greatest poets, but that the *Aeneid* and *The Divine Comedy* are the works, within the European tradition, which embody most comprehensively the particular qualities of the classic.

"There is no classic in English," Eliot says. Not that this is cause for tears: it is merely a statement that the particular relations among a people, a language, and a writer which constitute a classic are not to be found in any period of the English language. Eliot does not mention the American language in this lecture, but there is no reason to think that any work of American literature meets the three requirements of the classic. So if we speak of the American classics, as I do, we must use the word more liberally than Eliot does, and remind ourselves from time to time that our use of it is indeed concessive. This may guard us against overvaluing a work merely because it satisfies our social prejudices. It may also help us to understand why some books are privileged in a society and others are not.

It follows from Eliot's argument and the descriptions that accompany it that it is no longer possible to write a classic: the conditions can't be met. Eliot did not say this, but the classic is precisely and comprehensively what is no longer possible.[3] Goethe exemplifies what was no longer possible even for Goethe. *Provincialism* is Eliot's word for the disability, as it was Matthew Arnold's. The tone of the center, in Arnold's phrase, was not possible: there was no center. After the classics, there are only books, films, TV shows, and the Internet. The classics of American literature are by definition relative classics: there is no possibility of maturity, comprehensiveness, universality. But it may be useful to change the terminology, in the hope not of removing the disability but of introducing another perspective. In *L'Etre et l'événement* Alain Badiou distinguishes between the positivity of mere being and the actuality of events. A human life becomes an event when an act is radical or inaugural, when it impels everything that follows. The classics in American literature, relative classics as they are, are events, distinct from the mere being and succession of other books, good, bad, and mediocre. As events, they are privileged, even if the privilege is equivocal. What I mean by equivocal may be indicated by a linguistic point. Slavoj Zizek has remarked that the Russian language often has two words for what we westerners would consider the same referent: one word designates the ordinary meaning, and the other a more ethically charged or "absolute" use:

> There is *istina,* the common notion of truth as adequacy to facts; and (usually capitalized) *Pravda,* the absolute Truth also designating the ethically committed ideal Order of the Good. There is *svoboda,* the ordinary freedom to do as we like within the existing social order; and *volja,* the more metaphysically charged absolute drive to follow one's will up to self-destruction. . . . There is *gosudarstvo,* the state in its ordinary administrative aspects; and *derzhava,* the State as the unique agency of absolute Power.[4]

Lionel Trilling's distinction between sincerity and authenticity comes into a similar context: sincerity is the ordinary decent practice of one's life, authenticity is a far more demanding criterion. The difference is hardly clear in a dim light: it arises only if you invoke the supreme perspective. A similar distinction is operative in other languages, as between *tempus* and *aevum,* and between *futur* and *avenir.* But the situation is equivocal because one is, at any given moment, hovering between the ordinary meaning and the exalted or absolute meaning. Ordinary life is not respectful of absolutes, but there are some occasions—of crises, or even of anniversaries—when the higher question can't be put off.

Any one of the American classics is a cultural event, in Badiou's terms; it impels other events only less radical. And it is such an event, regardless of the aesthetic judgment one might make upon it. *Leaves of Grass* is an event, even though Quentin Anderson and (I suppose) other readers think it is a sinister book. The attitude a particular reader takes toward a classic may be reverent or impious. Reverent—here Zizek's note on the Russian language comes in—if the reader subscribes to the aura that surrounds the book, even among those who have not read it. Impious, if the reader rejects every instance of aura precisely because he or she suspects the imputed force of radiance; as one might detest the State while continuing to obey traffic lights and pay one's taxes.

What distinguishes a classic, at least in a concessive sense of the word, is that, to use a phrase of Alfred North Whitehead's given further currency by Frank Kermode, it is "patient of interpretation in terms of our interests." This is not a test as severe as Eliot's. Kermode means that such a work persists, through the many different interpretations of it: "I think there is a substance that prevails, however powerful the agents of change; that *King Lear,* underlying a thousand dispositions, subsists in change, prevails by being patient of interpretation."[5]

It makes a difficulty that this is an essentialist argument, requiring a distinction between the work in its presumed essence and the force of manifold dispositions in which it is found from time to time and from person to person. It also implies that another work—it is a mark of its not being a classic—demands to be interpreted in a particular way and does not survive the rough magic of different interpretations. I think that is true. *Uncle Tom's*

Cabin is not a classic: it asks to be read in a particular spirit. If you read it in a different spirit, it becomes an absurd book, though its historical impact in its time is still to be acknowledged.

3

It is a quality of the American classics that they have survived, for more than a hundred years, many dispositions: neglect, contempt, indifference, willful readings, excess of praise, hyperbole. There are formidably dismissive accounts of Whitman and Thoreau. I know some well-qualified readers who have no time for *The Scarlet Letter*. There are critics who would praise *Moby-Dick* if they could decide what kind of book they were praising. The question of canonicity arises on the margin of the classics. Some critics set themselves up as canonists and work to enforce or change the canon to satisfy their convictions. There are other critics who have no quarrel with the canon as it has emerged from the conflict of values in the general culture: they are willing to wait for the verdicts of this culture without intervening in the process. I think of D. H. Lawrence, R. P. Blackmur, Kenneth Burke, John Crowe Ransom, Allen Tate, and Frank Kermode as such critics. They are rarely found demanding that the merits of a neglected book be recognized and the canon changed in its favor. They assume that time will sufficiently tell. They may also be impressed by the fact that changes in fashion and style occur with some frequency and that one's sense of the literary scene loses its air of punctuality and rectitude after a few years. The way of the canonists is more aggressive. If you have canonist ambitions, you don't say "this is important," you say "this, not that, is important." Among the major modern poets and critics, Eliot and Pound were canonists, Yeats, Frost, and Stevens were not. Eliot and Pound wanted to change the world and to start by changing literature, or at least by changing the set of considerations with which readers habitually read it. A change of emphasis would help: admire Cavalcanti rather than Petrarch, to begin with. Eliot for a time tried to shift the emphasis of favor from Milton to Shakespeare, Donne, and George Herbert. F. R. Leavis was a canonist in *Revaluation; New Bearings in English Poetry; D. H. Lawrence, Novelist; The Living Principle;* and *Anna Karenina and Other Essays*. He wanted readers to approach modern poetry with Eliot and Pound in view as the crucial poets and Hopkins (rather than Tennyson or Browning) as the enabling figure in Victorian poetry. The fact that Leavis's convictions changed from Eliot to Lawrence and, at the end, from Lawrence to Tolstoy does not void his canonist fervor. I. A. Richards was a canonist in the sense that he demanded that literature be answerable to the disclosures of science, and he dismissed Yeats's early poems—not *The Tower* and *The Winding Stair and Other Poems*—for failing that test or not recognizing that the test was imperative. William Empson's canonist zeal was oblique: he favored poems that told stories and he set aside the heritage of Symbolism as a feeble thing, though he saw the merit of Eliot and Yeats when he thought they transcended their Symbolist origins. Yvor Winters dismissed Emerson, Whitman, and Hart Crane as irrationalists:

they could not think, or preferred not to think. Nineteenth-century American poetry for Winters amounted to Frederick G. Tuckerman, Jones Very, and a few of Emily Dickinson's poems. No twentieth-century poet, apparently, could survive comparison with Valéry. Philip Larkin was a canonist who maintained that the Modernism we associate with Eliot and Pound was a regrettable diversion, and that the genuine tradition of English poetry recognizes Hardy as incomparably the greatest modern poet. Harold Bloom has argued—or at least declared—that American poetry comes out of Emerson's overcoat and that the crucial poets are Whitman, Stevens, and whatever later poets acknowledge their agonistic kinship with these. Hugh Kenner argued that modern American poetry can be appreciated only by contrast with English poetry. English poetry received its distinctive character from its service to the Elizabethan theater. This has not been all gain. There are expressive possibilities in Chaucer and Langland which have never been developed in English poetry because the Elizabethan theater found no use for them. When Shakespeare and Marlowe wrote for the theater, they did not take their bearings from the penurious appearances on the stage; they provoked audiences to dream or imagine beyond those appearances. Those who saw a performance of Marlowe's *Dr. Faustus* saw a painted boy walking across the stage pretending to be Helen of Troy: what they heard—"Was this the face that launched a thousand ships?"—sent their minds dreaming of beautiful women, far-off seas, and ancient names. Kenner maintained that English ears, tuned to Shakespearean resonances, could not hear the poems of Marianne Moore and William Carlos Williams as poetry at all. No resonance, no reverberation, therefore no poetry. But the American language, according to Kenner, found its employment in service not to a national theater but to the institutions of sermon and pamphlet. More pamphlet than sermon. Resonance would have been a distraction, the main need being the application of intelligence to the matter in hand. Donne's "A bracelet of bright hair about the bone" is in unison with the Elizabethan theater, even though it was not written for the stage. It could not have appeared in an American poem. Pound was the greatest modern poet in English—or rather in American—because he saw what needed to be done and the nature of the necessary language, a language to direct the force of intelligence from one exemplary object of attention to the next. That is why Williams called Moore's poem "Marriage" an anthology of transit, a force of mind driving forward from one consideration to the next, not a set of cadences inviting the reader to rest upon a flourish of magniloquence. George Herbert's "Prayer" (I) is an English poem not only because Herbert was an Englishman but because it emphasizes the easy separateness of each of its phrases, easy because each phrase is an approximate description of prayer, subject to the unity and comprehensiveness of the final one, "something understood." Similarly, in Book VII of *Paradise Lost* the copiousness of the created universe is equably folded in the seventh day's rest—"Now resting, blessed and hallowed the sev'nth day" (line 592), the "Filial Power" enjoying the music of his accomplishment. This is "English poetry." But in American literature, as in Thoreau and Whitman, the entities invoked are there not for the gratification with which we recognize them but so that the poetic mind can be seen moving through them. Unity and comprehensiveness are internalized, posited in the writer's mind, the agent of transit. Thoreau and Whitman are confident that they can turn the otherwise dry facts of nature and culture into truths, fables, and myths, usually calling them democratic or American. The poetry-making faculty is the poet's imagination, not the mere inventory of what is objectively there. (These latter are my evidences, not Kenner's, but they cohere with his.) It followed, and propelled Kenner's canonist ambition, that the proper name for our time is the Pound Era and that Pound's legacy to American poets is Objectivism, its chief adepts being Moore, Williams, Charles Olson, Louis Zukofsky, and George Oppen. When Kenner wrote of other poets, including Yeats and Eliot, he construed them in relation to Pound, and diagnosed that relation as partial at best, hobbled through misunderstanding and allegiance to one version of Symbolism or another.

Sometimes the canonist ambition is pursued by reiterating the favorite names, as in Helen Vendler's books. I don't recall any book in which Vendler sets out a theory of poetry or a set of principles such that they are best fulfilled in her chosen poets. She is mainly interested in lyric poetry, which she thinks of and listens to as the voice of the soul, "the self when it is alone with itself, when its socially constructed characteristics (race, class, color, gender, sexuality) are felt to be in abeyance."[6] Why and when they are felt to be in abeyance, or how they could be, Vendler does not say. Nor does she say what the soul is doing when it is soliloquizing: is it doing what Emerson says one's genius is doing? Vendler has not explained how her lyric sense of poetry is fulfilled in the poems of Jorie Graham and Rita Dove and not, apparently, in those of Anthony Hecht, Richard Howard, John Hollander, or James Schuyler, poets who do not appear in her *Harvard Book of Contemporary American Poetry*. She may have excellent reasons, but she has not given them. Her method is to keep naming the chosen poets and commenting on their most telling poems. She has helped us to read Graham's "The Phase After History" by remarking how it is constructed, what goes with what, but she has not explained how its parts being put together in that way culminate in a major poem.

I have little canonist ambition. I am glad that *Their Eyes Were Watching God, The Awakening,* and "The Yellow Wallpaper" are now widely read, though I wish that additions to the canon were made on aesthetic rather than on ideological grounds. I would like to see Kenneth Burke's *Towards a Better Life* added to the canon of American fiction, but I am not impelled by such motives.

4

But critics don't make a canon. A canon is made not by critics or by common readers but by writers. Some writers are crucial to other writers: no particular writers matter very much to common readers. If common readers had their way, Stephen King, Mary Higgins Clark, and Tom Clancy would be among the canonical writers. They aren't. A canon is a list of books that writers have found inspiring. I'll give three instances. If Ezra Pound had his way, American education would attend to the proposition that "a national American culture existed from 1770 till at least 1861." He was not thrilled by the arrival of the *Mayflower* or the culture of New England Puritanism. Jonathan Edwards might as well not have been born. The values on which American culture should act are those expressed in the correspondence between Thomas Jefferson and John Adams in the years of reconciliation after their disagreements:

> From 1760 to 1826 two civilized men lived and to a considerable extent reigned in America. They did not feel themselves isolated phenomena. They were not by any means shrunk into a clique or dependent on mutual admiration, or on clique estimation. . . . In 170 years the United States have at no time contained a more civilized "world" than that comprised by the men to whom Adams and Jefferson wrote and from whom they received private correspondence.[7]

If Pound had written an ABC of American Reading, it would have started with Jefferson and Adams and continued with the best historians and scientists, Thomas Hart Benton and Martin

Van Buren for politics, Henry James eminent among the novelists, Thoreau and Louis Agassiz representing the morality of paying attention, and Whitman (with misgiving) the only classic poet worth reading. Emerson, Melville, and Mark Twain would probably not have come into the reckoning.

A second instance: William Carlos Williams, close to Pound and just as committed to history and its regions. In "The Writers of the American Revolution," "The American Background," and *In the American Grain* Williams lays out a syllabus of interests based not on habit but cognition, "the strange phosphorus of the life, nameless under an old misappellation."[8] Nothing like an encyclopedia is intended, though the names are many: Columbus, Cortez, Ponce de Leon, De Soto, Raleigh, the *Mayflower,* Puritans who "looked black at the world and damning its perfections praised a zero in themselves."[9] More to be attended to: Cotton Mather's *Magnalia,* Thomas Morton's *New English Canaan,* Père Sebastian Rasles, Daniel Boone, Parkman on the Jesuits in America, The Maypole of Merry Mount (May Day 1627), Washington, Franklin, John Paul Jones, Burr, Sam Houston, Poe (the most resolute appreciation of him I have seen), then Lincoln. "The Writers of the American Revolution" is a long footnote to *In the American Grain,* and gives further names: James Otis, Samuel Adams, Franklin, Tom Paine, Jefferson, Freneau, Crèvecoeur's *Letters from an American Farmer,* William Bartram's *Travels,* John Adams. "The American Background" gives the theory of Williams's syllabus and reasons for his exclusions or diminishments, notably of Emerson, whose "slightly hackneyed gentility" caused him to rise "into a world of thought which he believed to be universal only because he couldn't see whence it had arisen."[10] The five classics don't get much play; they are not Poundian or otherwise Enlightenment or Objectivist.

Robert Lowell's lists are all-over-the-library, but his emphasis is on the New England tradition, as he engages with it in the plays of *The Old Glory* and *Benito Cereno* and many poems, notably "The Quaker Graveyard in Nantucket," "Mr. Edwards and the Spider," "At the Indian Killer's Grave," "After the Surprising Conversions," "Hawthorne," "Jonathan Edwards in Western Massachusetts," "For the Union Dead," "Henry and Waldo," and the two Thoreau poems. It is not my business to say anything about this body of work, except to note that it brings forward the old glory not for redemption but for a bearing distinctly personal and exacerbated and therefore cultural. It is not Lowell's fault that the American classics were written by five white men, and that publishers in New York and Boston—themselves white men—largely determined that this should be the case. It was not necessary for Lowell to love the glory he wrestled with, but only to be gripped by it. Blackmur said of *Land of Unlikeness* that there is nothing loved in it "unless it be its repellence," and he suggested as reason that in Lowell's early poems "logic lacerates the vision and vision turns logic to zealotry."[11] That seems to me to be near the mark, and to speak to Lowell's poems New Englandly.

5

Why should anyone read these five books? They are not self-evidently the best books in American literature. When I read for pleasure—especially for the pleasure of discriminating among values—I am far more likely to read *The Waste Land, The Portrait of a Lady, Life Studies, Notes Toward a Supreme Fiction, Absalom! Absalom!, Blood Meridian, Towards a Better Life,* or *Stories in an Almost Classical Mode* than *The Scarlet Letter;* more inclined to read *The Education of Henry Adams, Mont-Saint-Michel and Chartres, What We Talk About When We Talk About Love, The Pilgrim Hawk,* or *A Sport and a Pastime* than *Walden.* But there are at least two good reasons for reading the five: they make available to readers—or have a good chance of doing so—a shared cultural experience, something in which American society is otherwise impoverished. Those who read *Stories in an Almost Classical Mode* are merely individuals here and there, they are not a people or representatives of a people, they don't hold in common the imaginative experience the book offers. The five classics also put in question the otherwise facile ideology of individualism on which American culture complacently prides itself. More to the point: they ask to be read deliberately. Reading is a slow, private act. It is not surprising that many Americans have given up reading and take their instruction, information, and entertainment from TV. *Reading at Risk: A Survey of Literary Reading in America,* a recent report of the National Endowment for the Arts, offers evidence—based on interviews with more than seventeen thousand witnesses—that reading literature declined from 1982 to 2002 in all age groups: by 17 percent among those aged eighteen through twenty-four, nearly as drastic a drop through age forty-four, and smaller declines—but still, declines—among the middle-aged and elderly.[12] Television and photography have a far more immediate relation—not necessarily a more mature relation—to one's mind than reading has. The photographs of the abuse and humiliation of Iraqi prisoners by American soldiers—a few of them published in newspapers and magazines but more on the Internet—were far more effective internationally than any discursive account of the conditions at Abu Ghraib and other prisons would have been. The shock of having one's mind suffused by images was far more compelling than words. Reading a book is a different experience, slower, more thoughtful, more arduous.

6

The canon of American literature is Emersonian. If you start with Emerson, you soon come to Thoreau, Whitman, and Hawthorne. Hawthorne leads to Melville by kinship and difference. The scene of these relations extends from Concord, Massachusetts, to Camden, New Jersey. Emily Dickinson is not at hand: no single poem has been given the status of a classic. Emerson's context includes Margaret Fuller and Louisa May Alcott. Mark Twain arrived later and from another region. California and other parts of the country have good books but not classics. We keep coming back to Emerson, mainly because some version of his individualism drives the five books to which I attribute relative classic status. Emerson is not himself a classic writer; no book, essay, or poem of his has entered into the common discourse (if there is such a thing). *Representative Men, English Traits, Essays: First Series,* and *Essays: Second Series* have not become parts of the common culture (so far as there is such a thing). Emerson is a great personage, a great enabler; he is remarkable mainly as incentive and provocation, as the cause of writers greater than he is: that is why we find him everywhere, not merely in himself and his writings. No book of his is a classic, but there are thrilling sentences, endlessly productive. He is most of the context of these five books, even when they have nothing directly to say of him. So I think it is well to begin with Emerson and to concentrate on one of his most vigorous lectures, "The American Scholar."

But I should explain without further ado why I so regularly invoke the critics of an earlier generation, from Eliot to Empson. This is partly why I have called the book a personal essay: it is a chapter of autobiography. Eliot, Leavis, Empson, Winters, Blackmur, and Burke were the critics who defined the context in which I first read the American classics. That their literary criticism has been forgotten is not my fault. The period of criticism from James's Prefaces to Empson's *The Structure of Complex Words* marks the most concentrated attention to literary, social, and political issues in my lifetime. These include questions of education, as in Richard Hoggart's *The Uses of Literacy,* the impingement of popular culture on high culture, the search for qualified readers in the midst of the "broad-backed public," as James called it, the attempt to maintain literature in conditions largely amounting to waste, the life of the imagination, independent despite every assault on its independence, the relation between the arts and the general culture, the practices of reading. The critics I read most warmly are those who worried these and other issues and brought them to the state of conversation. They seem to me more conversible than their successors: at least I feel that I have been able to talk to them and to listen to them, in a sense in which it has proved difficult to listen to their successors, X and Y. I have no quarrel otherwise with X and Y.

I

Emerson and "The American Scholar"

> Perhaps you have begun to realize how the pretension of consciousness to constitute itself is the most formidable obstacle to the idea of revelation.
>
> —Paul Ricoeur

I

On August 31, 1837, Emerson delivered the annual Phi Beta Kappa lecture at Harvard under the title "The American Scholar." He was not the first choice of the society for its lecturer that year: the invitation came to him only when Jonathan Wainright withdrew his acceptance. Nor was he an especially suitable choice. The Phi Beta Kappa lecture was the occasion each year on which Harvard Unitarianism showed the desperate remnant of its force and confronted its Transcendentalist, Idealist, and otherwise Romantic opponents. Emerson could not have been expected to fight for the Unitarian cause, even though he had not yet spoken in public in favor of Transcendentalism, as he was to speak for it in January 1842. The chapter on "Idealism" in Emerson's first book, *Nature* (1836), was equivocal: you could take it as asserting that the natural world has whatever meaning the human mind gives it, and no other. Nature is fortunate in having the human mind redeem it from nullity. But for the mind that engages with it, nature would not be worth talking about or living in. On the other hand, you have to accept that the natural world is there, so it must have at least the claim of existing for a putative reason. Emerson veers between these considerations, subject only to his insistence that nature is inferior to mind. He never asks himself Leibniz's question: why is there something rather than nothing? But in that silence *Nature* can be quoted to any purpose.

Emerson's mind remained religious, though theologically unexacting if not etiolated. On September 9, 1832, he announced his resignation from the Unitarian ministry, and while he continued to speak now and then from a pulpit, he was committed to move from sermon to lecture as the form of his public career. His resignation marks a significant moment in the decision of American culture to do without a religious myth, except for the vaguely religious one of America as "redeemer nation." In the event, Emerson's lecture on "The American Scholar," like the one he gave the following year to the senior class of the Harvard Divinity School, and his more famous lecture in 1839 on "Self-Reliance," established the secular turn of his mind, but without any trace of Materialism. Nevertheless, many of those who listened to "The American Scholar" were dismayed. Fifty years later, Henry James was amused "at the spectacle of a body of people among whom the author of 'The American Scholar' and of the Address of 1838 at the Harvard Divinity College passed for profane, and who failed to see that [Emerson] only gave his plea for the spiritual life the advantage of a brilliant expression. . . . They were so provincial," James said, "as to think that brilliancy came ill-recommended, and they were shocked at his ceasing to care for the prayer and the sermon." "They should have perceived," James continued, "that he *was* the prayer and the sermon: not in the least a seculariser, but in his own subtle insinuating way a sanctifier."[1] But the last thing the Phi Beta Kappa Society wanted from Emerson was a display of his subtle insinuating ways. The members knew well enough that he had abandoned them. His tone was edifying, but it was not religious in any sense a Unitarian would accept, even though to be a Unitarian was to be tepid by default if not on principle.

The topic Emerson chose was a standard one. Several of his predecessors had lectured on the responsibilities of the intellectual life or the nature of learning in a country not much noted for it. Emerson referred to "a people too busy to give to letters any more." In the first minute or two of the lecture he expressed the hope that "the sluggard intellect of this continent" might "look from under its iron lids, and fill the postponed expectation of the world with something better than the exertions of mechanical skill." The future, as he conjured it, was his favorite tense. Meanwhile, he acknowledged that the scholar must put up with many disabilities. Instead of being able to speak boldly, he must be content to stammer:

> Long he must stammer in his speech; often forego the living for the dead. Worse yet, he must accept,—how often! poverty and solitude. For the ease and pleasure of treading the old road, accepting the fashions, the education, the religion of society, he takes the cross of making his own, and, of course, the self-accusation, the faint heart, the frequent uncertainty and loss of time, which are the nettles and tangling vines in the way of the self-relying and self-directed; and the state of virtual hostility in which he seems to stand to society, and especially to educated society.

Where would the scholar find consolation? Only in knowing that he exercises "the highest functions of human nature."[2]

Who is this scholar, this martyr who takes up the cross? Emerson speaks of him as "Man Thinking," "the designated intellect." But that is to imagine him in his right or ideal state. "In the degenerate state, when the victim of society, he tends to become a mere thinker, or, still worse, the parrot of other men's thinking."[3] He is the victim of society when he merely thinks in the forms prescribed for him, which are partial or mean forms by definition. Henry James, in the essay from which I have quoted, is still wondering who on earth this scholar could be or could have been:

> Charming to many a reader, charming yet ever so slightly droll, will remain Emerson's frequent invocation of the "scholar": there is such a friendly vagueness and

> convenience in it. It is of the scholar that he expects all the heroic and uncomfortable things, the concentrations and relinquishments, that make up the noble life. We fancy this personage looking up from his book and armchair a little ruefully and saying, "Ah, but why *me* always and only? Why so much of me, and is there no one else to share the responsibility?"[4]

James could only assume that by *scholar* Emerson meant "the cultivated man, the man who has had a liberal education," one who was distinguished by having some relation to literature, a relation James noted as being a privileged association in Emerson's time. But that is a small interpretation. James did not appreciate that to Emerson the chief attribute of the scholar was that he did not yet exist; he existed only in Emerson's yearning vision of him, and in his demand that such a person would emerge, the need of him being acute. Stanley Cavell correctly refers to the American Scholar as "Emerson's vision of our not yet thinking."[5] Perhaps Emerson himself, as sage and prophet, was the only living exemplar of the scholar, but he could hardly make that claim for himself. He had to speak of the scholar as if there were such a being, or at least as if an adumbration of such could be invoked, even in the degradation of an ideal possibility. Otherwise he might just as well throw up his hands and confess that he was dreaming.

But Emerson's scholar exists only as an idea, like Wallace Stevens's "major man" in *Notes Toward a Supreme Fiction:* "It does not follow that major man is man." Man and the idea of man are discontinuous projects. As a poet, Stevens was of Emerson's fellowship, but he had come a long way from him in one respect:

> From this the poem springs: that we live in a place
> That is not our own and, much more, not ourselves
> And hard it is in spite of blazoned days.[6]

Stevens wanted to believe that the place we live in is not only our own but ourselves, cognate to our imaginations, and he wrote his poems as evidences that this felicity was at least possible. Emerson was closer to the Transcendentalism of Kant, who maintained in reply to John Locke that there are ideas, "imperative forms" as Emerson called them, forms that did not come from sensory experience but through which sensory experience was acquired.[7] The world is not merely the tissue of entities it seems to be: it is, from the point of view of Idealism, "this shadow of the soul, or *other me*."[8] Or so Emerson needed to believe. The idealist makes one's consciousness account for the whole of one's experience.

It is a cardinal axiom of Emerson's sense of experience that he invoked the idea of Man without coming to particular men or women. "It is one of those fables," he said, "which, out of an unknown antiquity, convey an unlooked-for wisdom, that the gods, in the beginning, divided Man into men, that he might be more helpful to himself; just as the hand was divided into fingers, the better to answer its end." Emerson interpreted the fable to sustain "a doctrine ever new and sublime; that there is One Man,—present to all particular men only partially, or through one faculty; and that you must take the whole society to find the whole man." Man "is not a farmer, or a professor, or an engineer, but he is all." He is "priest, and scholar, and statesman, and producer, and soldier." In the "*divided* or social state, these functions are parceled out to individuals, each of whom aims to do his stint of the joint work, whilst each other performs his."[9] But Emerson deplores this parceling out. At the very least, each of us should retain a sense of the whole of which he or she is one part. This good intention soon became a lost cause. Later nineteenth century practice decided that one's only hope of being effective consisted in one's being a specialist, forgetting about the whole man, relegating to one's hours of abstraction any concern for Man as distinct from men. Max Weber accepted this decision in his lecture on "Science as a Vocation," and the world has regarded the question as settled.

In "The American Scholar" Emerson speaks of the several conditions and influences which bear upon the scholar as if each were to be understood in terms of philosophic Idealism. The first influence is Nature, the continuity and circuit of natural life. But nature also includes the little society of men and women, conversing. Emerson believes that the natural world is a system of analogies, and that the law of Nature coincides with the prior law of the human mind: nature answers to the soul, part by part. It is crucial that each of us discovers that the law of nature is the law of one's own mind. This is the justification of a scholar's search for further knowledge. "So much of nature as he is ignorant of, so much of his own mind does he not yet possess." The purpose of scholarship, according to Emerson, is not the elucidation of nature as an objective entity or structure independent of you and me but as the correlative constitution of one's own mind. "The ancient precept, 'Know thyself,' and the modern precept, 'Study nature,' become at last one maxim."[10]

The second influence on the mind of the scholar is "the mind of the Past," but Emerson gives a light if not a light-hearted account of this; he does not weigh its burden. Indeed, he shows himself "a little provincial" at this point, in the sense of provincialism that Eliot described in "What Is a Classic?" "In our age," Eliot said, "when men seem more than ever prone to confuse wisdom with knowledge, and knowledge with information, and to try to solve problems of life in terms of engineering, there is coming into existence a new kind of provincialism which perhaps deserves a new name." Keeping the old name, Eliot continued: "It is a provincialism, not of space, but of time; one for which history is merely the chronicle of human devices which have served their turn and been scrapped, one for which the world is the property solely of the living, a property in which the dead hold no shares."[11]

"We are not children of time," Emerson said in one of his early lectures on history. "All the facts of history pre-exist in the mind as laws."[12] It would be difficult to convince the parents of a soldier killed at the Somme or of a child bombed to death in Dresden that the facts of history are to be respected only as psychological laws. Emerson relegates the chronicle of human devices which have served their turn by finding them in books, where they can easily be allowed not to impinge. He ascribes value not to books as such, as products or vehicles where claims are made, but to the minds that wrote them. He deplores the congealment of those minds that occurs when institutions turn them into books, books into libraries, libraries into conformities. "Meek young men grow up in libraries, believing it their duty to accept the views, which Cicero, which Locke, which Bacon, have given, forgetful that Cicero, Locke, and Bacon were only young men in libraries, when they wrote these books." Books "are for nothing but to inspire." We should read them—especially books of history and natural science—to learn what is already known and to see the forms, or some of them, that genius and creative spirit have taken. But "I had better never see a book, than to be warped by its attraction clean out of my own orbit, and made a satellite rather than a system." Even the genius of another should be resisted. "Genius is always sufficiently the enemy of genius by overinfluence." The literatures of every nation, Emerson says, "bear me witness. The English dramatic poets have Shakespearized now for two hundred years." So there is a creative way of reading, according to which readers do not allow themselves to be subdued by what they read. They remain their own seers. "Books are for the scholar's idle times. When he can read God directly, the hour is too precious to be wasted in other men's transcripts of their readings."[13]

The clue to Emerson's extravagances, in this part of his lecture, is his belief that we can read God directly. But what does that mean? It can only mean that we can read ourselves, that each of us can read his or her individual genius, and thereby intuit the comprehensive genius of which our little genius is a fragment. Stevens writes, in "Final Soliloquy of the Interior Paramour": "We say God and the imagination are one."[14] This allows for the possibility that we may be wrong: we may be found wrong. But meanwhile there is evidently some consolation to be felt in the saying. Emerson also says consoling things, and admonitory things; says them in notebook, lecture, and printed book. But he presents a claim to the truth of what he says, not merely the consolation of saying it. His claim is predicated on the force—or at least the hypothetical force—of what he calls "the one thing in the world of value, . . . the active soul."[15] Books are a nuisance when we let them get in the way of that soul.

The third influence on the scholar of which Emerson speaks is the common notion that because scholars are speculative people they must be recluses, valetudinarians. On the contrary, Emerson declares for action in the world. "The true scholar grudges every opportunity of action past by, as a loss of power."[16] In saying as much, Emerson had to resist his own disposition. He was not, by nature, given to the gregariousness of taking up causes or acting directly in the world. It was typical of his Idealism to reduce Action to Attitude, taking up a stance in advance of its occasion and sometimes letting the occasion go by. We normally find him in a state of incipience, his animation held in suspense. It took him several years to work up the conviction required to speak out against slavery in the American South; till August 1, 1844, to be specific, when he spoke in Concord to mark the tenth anniversary of the emancipation of slaves in the British West Indies. In later years he sometimes—but rarely—overcame his reluctance to join other people in helping a just cause. In May 1851 he denounced the Fugitive Slave Law and attacked his one-time hero Daniel Webster for supporting it. On March 7, 1854, he spoke again against the Fugitive Slave Law, and in 1855 he spoke with even greater force against slavery. But in these speeches he worked despite his inclinations and against his native grain.

Emerson was most at one with himself when he was describing the active soul and demanding that it come forth. In "The American Scholar" he says that the duties of the scholar "are such as become Man Thinking." Again he distinguishes between Man Thinking and mere men. The best that a man may strive for is to achieve "self-trust." He is "to feel all confidence in himself, and to defer never to the popular cry. . . . Let him not quit his belief that a popgun is a popgun, though the ancient and the honorable of the earth affirm it to be the crack of doom." If he trusts himself, he will discover that his feelings are universal. Exerting all confidence in himself, the scholar will eventually find "that in going down into the secrets of his own mind, he has descended into the secrets of all minds." So it is a libel, according to Emerson, that we are come too late in the world, "that the world was finished a long time ago." He refers to "the discontent of the literary class" and thinks it "a mere announcement of the fact, that they find themselves not in the state of mind of their fathers, and regret the coming state as untried." Emerson will have none of this ruefulness, none of the feeling that the time is out of joint. "As the world was plastic and fluid in the hands of God, so it is ever to so much of his attributes as we bring to it." The main enterprise of the world "for splendor, for extent," Emerson maintains, "is the upbuilding of a man."[17] But a man, rightly considered, comprehends "the particular natures of all men." So Emerson starts with Man, the idea of man, a part of God's supreme consciousness, and in that respect the type of all men. It is a version of Perfectionism. God is not separate from man, but is man construed as divine.

Emerson brings "The American Scholar" to an end by offering several reasons for being of good cheer. He is not dismayed to be living in a philosophic or reflective age. He is pleased that writers are taking an interest in ordinary life, ordinary people: "instead of the sublime and beautiful; the near, the low, the common. . . . The literature of the poor, the feelings of the child, the philosophy of the street, the meaning of household life, are the topics of the time. It is a great stride." He means the literature of Goldsmith, Burns, Cowper, Goethe, Wordsworth, and Carlyle; while he speaks with distaste of the works of Pope, Johnson, and Gibbon. And he makes particularly approving mention of Swedenborg, one of his "representative men," for attempting "to engraft a purely philosophical Ethics on the popular Christianity of his time." Then he reverts to his favorite theme, the "new importance given to the single person," so that "each man shall feel the world is his, and man shall treat with man as a sovereign state with a sovereign state." The lecture becomes a poet's declaration of American independence from Britain, from Europe. "We have listened too long to the courtly muses of Europe."[18] Emerson ends with a prophecy, an appeal to the future, and to great expression as its form. He cannot foresee Whitman, though we know that Whitman's *Leaves of Grass* was the first fulfillment of Emerson's prophecy.

2

I have been asking: who is, or was, the American Scholar? But a more fundamental question is: who is the human being who in principle precedes him? Who is this wondrous being, and how did he come to be such? When we refer to individuality or to the ideology of individualism which acts upon Emerson's auspices, who is the origin and beneficiary of such terms? And what is the democracy in which he or she supposedly participates?

Emerson's individual is a nominal entity; not Tom, Dick, Harry, or Mary, but the proclaimed possibility of each. The status of that possibility is a question. Cavell says that "Emerson's writing works out the conditions for my recognizing my difference from others as a function of my recognizing my difference from myself."[19] But he does not appear to see how destructive such a recognition is. Emmanuel Levinas would denounce it as the worst act of Idealism, the reduction of someone to me, even if the me is achieved by self-division and critique. Individualism is the quiet name for egotism, the claim upon which an assertion of individuality is made, in principle and only in principle. Emerson's saving grace—which he seems to stand in need of—is that his repeated insistence upon individualism is an insistence upon a process, not an achievement or a conclusion. His praise of "'the infinitude of the private man'"—from the Journals of April 1840—is, as Cavell puts it, "not a praise of any existing man or men but an announcement of the process of individuation (an interpretation of perfectionism) before which there are no individuals, hence no humanity, no society."[20] The self is not—though Emerson sometimes writes as if it were—an entity stable while the going is good and for as long as you pay attention to it: it is, properly speaking, a verb, not a noun, it denotes capacities in transition, a movement from one notional state of being to another, equally notional. It must be so, if only because Emerson had very little interest in people at large. He despised the masses he pointed to in *The Conduct of Life*. In "Uses of Great Men" he says that "enormous populations, if they be beggars, are disgusting, like moving cheese, like hills of ants, or of fleas—the more, the worse."[21] What would he say if he were brought on a visit to Calcutta or Harare? Even when he attacked the institution of slavery, he continued to think that black people were congenitally inferior: he had no more time for them than Thoreau had for Irish immigrants working on the

Fitchburg railway. But he held to the idea of individuality as an idea, and invoked the genius of each of us. "To believe your own thought, to believe that what is true for you in your private heart is true for all men,—that is genius."[22] It is also nonsense and vanity, if we think of people as the entities we see around us and in ourselves. To believe in your own thought is consistent with having no convictions other than the conviction of your genius. With that thought in mind, Emerson's talk of genius seems an empty formula, not redeemed by being rampant in American culture. You can have your genius, apparently, even if there is no producible evidence for your being anything but a lout or a fool. Tocqueville noted that many values proclaimed in America were similarly empty. "Society has nothing to fear or hope from another life; what is most important for it is not that all citizens should profess the true religion but that they should profess religion."[23] In 1930 John Dewey said of American religion that "nowhere in the world at any time has religion been so thoroughly respectable as with us, and so nearly totally disconnected from life."[24] That is why religion in America so easily presents itself as a genteel convention, a custom of social life; unless it draws attention to itself, as Islamic fundamentalism is said to do, and can be associated with hostility toward the United States. The only way of retaining Emerson's notion of individual genius is by deeming it visionary, a gesture toward a future state not at all resembling the one we have: if we think of it as saying only "In Our Next."

3

Emerson did not invent the ideology of individualism and self-reliance, though he bears the responsibility of making it charming to Americans. The conceit of self-creation has been a beguiling sentiment at least since Milton's Satan gave it the glamour of a heroic posture, however specious. But there are distinctions to be made. Charles Taylor has pointed out that it was Augustine who introduced "the inwardness of radical reflexivity"—in Taylor's phrase—and made it available to Western thought:

> The step was a fateful one, because we have certainly made a big thing of the first-person standpoint. The modern epistemological tradition from Descartes, and all that has flowed from it in modern culture, has made this standpoint fundamental—to the point of aberration, one might think. It has gone as far as generating the view that there is a special domain of "inner" objects available only from this standpoint; or the notion that the vantage point of the "I think" is somehow outside the world of things we experience.

It may appear that Augustine has much to answer for, but Taylor notes that Augustine did not present the "turn to the self in the first-person dimension" as an intrinsic value; he made it "crucial to our access to a higher condition—because in fact it is a step on our road back to God." Augustine "needs to be rescued from identification both with his successors and with his predecessors."

Taylor proposed to do this by placing Augustine between Plato and Descartes. "Augustine makes the step to inwardness . . . because it is a step towards God":

> The truth dwells within . . . and God is Truth. One way in which this shows itself is in our attempt to prove God's existence. Augustine offers us such a proof in the dialogue *On Free Will,* Book II. He tries to show his interlocutor that there is something higher than our reason, which thus deserves to be called God. The proof turns on the insight that reason recognizes that there is a truth which is criterial for it, i.e., a standard on which it regulates itself, which is not its own making, but beyond it and common to all.[25]

Emerson's individualism is different: it is an assertively intrinsic value, acknowledging no duty to a higher criterion. In this respect he differs also from Levinas. Levinas allows for an inner life, but he does not call it the soul as distinct from the self, a distinction that Yeats and others have made. But he ensures a place for it when one would hardly expect him to do so. "The inner life," he says in *Totality and Infinity,* "is the unique *way* for the real to exist as a plurality." Interiority constitutes an order in which "what is no longer possible historically remains always possible." But an event in my interiority can only be a substitute for what is no longer possible historically. Emerson often seems to claim that anything is possible historically and that that possibility is what is entailed by individualism. But there is no impulse in Emerson that corresponds to Levinas's insistence that "ethics precedes ontology."[26] Emerson encourages his readers to think that real history is the history of consciousness: there is one story and one story only. But he can't be blamed for the crassness of the ideology of consciousness, self-reliance, and individualism, if only because he tended to withdraw his credence from any concept or entity as soon as he had posited it. He also—very often—ignores its logical consequences. His positing a value was a sign that his relation to it was already equivocal or residual. Other people took him more literally than he took himself, and settled for his tenets, forgetting the misgiving with which Emerson shadowed them. Those readers followed him in every respect but the spirit in which he revised himself and disowned his certitude. So it became a short step for Americans to regard themselves as categorically destined to be exceptional, the chosen vehicle of redemption, justified in imposing their will upon others. Levinas was never open to that temptation. One can argue with his insistence that ethics precedes ontology, if only because it entails that philosophy should become ethics as Rorty and Habermas think it should become politics. But under any designation, consciousness in Levinas becomes conscience, and acts under the sign of responsibility. He has often quoted the passage in *The Brothers Karamazov* in which Alyosha says: "We are all responsible for everyone else, but I am more responsible than all the others." To this, Levinas added the words of the rabbi Israel Salander: "The material needs of my neighbour are my spiritual needs."[27] According to Levinas, self-creation, self-consciousness, individualism are not at all primary. The primary act is the one by which I address another person as "you." I ground my existence solely upon that act of acknowledgment, that saying. The essence of discourse is not political, as in Habermas, or psychological, as in Emerson, or even reciprocal, as in Buber's *I and Thou.* In Buber, I acknowledge you, and you in turn will acknowledge me. From this reciprocity, a community begins to form. That is not enough for Levinas. He accepts that reciprocity between persons is a good basis for the political order of citizens in a state, but according to *Totality and Infinity* and *Otherwise Than Being,* I should acknowledge you as an irreducible person whether you acknowledge me or not. As in love, one resigns oneself to the possibility of not being loved by the person one loves. It is only by acknowledging you that I come to be myself. Until I make that commitment, I can merely, in the sordid language of individualism, insist on being my sole self—my genius, in Emerson's term.

4

It is not at all self-evident that Emersonian individualism is compatible with democracy or indeed that it serves any particular ideology. Like Thoreau, Emerson fears and therefore affects to despise society. He gets over the logical problem of doing so by acknowledging the difference between the life he lives by thinking and the circumstantial life he otherwise lives. What he thinks, with the degree of independence available to thinking, is easily compatible with what he hopes: what he surmises is a future of his own devising. He has no need—and little inclination—to pay much attention to other people and their activities; as John Jay Chapman remarked, "If an inhabitant of another planet should visit the earth, he would receive, on the whole, a truer notion of human life by attending an Italian opera than he would by reading Emerson's volumes. He would learn from the Italian opera that there were two sexes; and this, after all, is probably the fact with which the education of such a stranger ought to begin."[28] Emerson is bound to regard society as a nuisance, an embodiment of the conformity he repudiates. What else could it be?

A good deal is at stake here, at least for Americans who want to proclaim not only democracy as such (which they can hardly claim to have invented) but specifically the American version of it (as the perfection of that Greek idea), and to present Emerson as its hero. George Kateb has made the most strenuous efforts in this direction, especially in two books, *The Inner Ocean: Individualism and Democratic Culture* (1992) and *Emerson and Self-Reliance* (2002). In both, he praises individualism by presenting it as the flowering of democracy: it is, in his view, a social value rather than a nuance of self-production or self-creation. It is embarrassing to his case that Emerson has no interest in providing professors of politics with a theory of society: in that respect they must look out for themselves. What provision has Emerson made for a self-reliant individual to work with others, Kateb rather daringly asks? The short answer is: none. That is not Emerson's concern.[29] Kateb has an interest in making Emersonian individualism sustain democracy, but it is a hopeless undertaking, except in the negative sense that no other political ideology is in any better state or could better enjoy Emerson's favor. Chapman is entirely justified in saying that "if a soul be taken and crushed by democracy till it utter a cry, that cry will be Emerson," and again that "while the radicals of Europe were revolting in 1848 against the abuses of a tyranny whose roots were in feudalism, Emerson, the great radical of America, the arch-radical of the world, was revolting against the evils whose roots were in universal suffrage."[30] There is no merit in eliding the severity of Emerson's insistences in the hope of making an American democrat. He was really an anarchist; necessarily so, since he cultivated the thrill of glorifying his own mind and refused to let any other consideration thwart him. You may think this a cheap thrill, as I do, but it was the only one that Emerson consistently enjoyed.

In "Self-Reliance" Emerson speaks of congenial voices as those we hear in solitude, "but they grow faint and inaudible as we enter into the world":

> Society everywhere is in conspiracy against the manhood of every one of its members. Society is a joint-stock company, in which the members agree, for the better securing of his bread to each shareholder, to surrender the liberty and culture of the eater. The virtue in most request is conformity. Self-reliance is its aversion.

> It loves not realities and creators, but names and customs.[31]

What Emerson seems to mean by aversion is one's practice of endless dissatisfaction, not only with society but with one's self. Cavell interprets it in this spirit: "Since Emerson also speaks of our living always with an unattained but attainable self, I understand him to mean that to have a self is always to be averse to one's attained self (in one's so far attained society); put otherwise, to conform to the self is to relinquish it."[32]

It follows that a self, for Emerson, is a splendid attribute, so long as we are not content to possess it but are always striving toward the next vision, its further far-off possibility. As a possession, it amounts to yet another instance of conformity.

Cavell has meditated further on what he calls aversive thinking, the kind in which one turns aside from the world and for that reason keeps in view the world from which one has turned aside. But he is not willing to rest with the standard interpretation of the sentences "The virtue in most request is conformity. Self-reliance is its aversion." He gives a different account of the passage:

> Naturally Emerson's critics take this to mean roughly that he is disgusted with society and wants no more to do with it. But the idea of self-reliance as the aversion of conformity figures each side in terms of the other, declares the issue between them as always joined, never settled. But then this is to say that Emerson's writing and

> his society are in an unending argument with one another—that is to say, he writes in such a way as to *place* his writing in his unending argument (such is his loyal opposition)—an unending turning away from one another, but for that exact reason a constant keeping in mind of one another, hence endlessly a turning *toward* one another.

This seems to me a quibble; it presents aversion as, in the end, a trivial act, merely postponed accommodation. The comparison of it to an endless conversation and to the loyal opposition one finds in the Mother of Parliaments has the effect of domesticating aversion and making it content with the exchange of attitudes, talk for the sake of talk. I interpret Cavell's reading of the word as a parliamentary attempt to make Emerson's thinking a social act, despite the many evidences that it is not. He is determined to make Emerson a participant in the world, perhaps even that unlikely person, a democrat. He can do this—or try to do it—only by construing conflict as fellowship, and disgust as the other side of affection. Asking himself whether Emersonian and Nietzschean perfectionism "is necessarily undemocratic," he resorts to the opportunistic claim that only in a democracy would one be likely to get away with it:

> I might put my thought this way: the particular disdain for official culture taken in Emerson and in Nietzsche (and surely in half the writers and artists in the one

> hundred and fifty years since "The American Scholar," or say since romanticism) is itself an expression of democracy and commitment to it. Timocrats do not produce, oligarchs do not commission, dictators do not enforce, art and culture that disgust them. Only within the possibility of democracy is one committed to living with, or against, such culture. This may well produce personal tastes and private choices that are, let us say, exclusive, even esoteric. Then my question is whether this exclusiveness might be not just tolerated but treasured by the friends of democracy.[33]

But disdain for official culture has to mean, in Emerson's case, disdain for democracy: it is the only official culture in place. It is true, but beside the point, that in a totalitarian state an Emerson would have to hold his tongue. True: conformity was exacted far more resolutely in Stalin's Soviet Union than in Roosevelt's United States—though even there to be of Japanese origin in 1942 and living in California was to find oneself interned without trial under Executive Order 9066. By Emerson's standards, the principle of conformity is enforced wherever there is an official culture, however genial its appearances are. That is the force of an ideology, it pretends that laws of society are laws of nature and therefore self-evidently justified.

Cavell and, much more blatantly, Kateb are notably complacent about the American character of the democracy they enjoy.

They have apparently forgotten that the regime of George W. Bush and John Ashcroft contrived not only to interpret the USA Patriot Act illiberally but to keep an American citizen, José Padilla, indefinitely in solitary confinement without charge. Not to speak of the use to which the Bush administration has put Guantánamo Bay. Admittedly, it was in 1990, long before the appointment of Ashcroft as attorney general, that Cavell professed himself as living "within a society characterized—it is a mark of my consent to say so—by good enough justice."[34] To which it is necessary to reply: there is never good enough justice.

It may be thought that I have moved away from Emerson's notion of the American Scholar, but I haven't. One passage in Emerson's lecture suggests that the scholar, if he were to come into existence, would be what we call "the public intellectual." Emerson says:

> In silence, in steadiness, in severe abstraction, let him hold by himself; add observation to observation, patient of neglect, patient of reproach; and bide his own time,—happy enough, if he can satisfy himself alone, that this day he has seen something truly. Success treads on every right step. For the instinct is sure, that prompts him to tell his brother what he thinks.[35]

That seems to endorse not necessarily the daily journalist with a few columns to fill or the armchair critic on television news programs, but the public intellectuals who do their jobs, teaching and researching and on occasions of public moment applying their intelligence to the issues in front of them. For many months after the attacks on the World Trade Center and the Pentagon on September 11, 2001, it looked as if public intellectuals had lapsed into silence. The Bush administration seemed to go on its way without criticism or interrogation. House and Senate were in intellectual and moral abeyance. To find any expression of interrogation or dissent, one had to read a few English newspapers and magazines—*The Guardian, The Independent, The London Review of Books*—and, a year later, two or three foreign books. Only gradually, and especially since early in 2004, when Osama bin Laden has not been found, "weapons of mass destruction" have not been discovered, and the aftermath of the invasion of Iraq continues to be a lethal mess: only now is it possible to read books and articles of intellectual and moral dissent in the United States. Even yet, the times are not auspicious for such interventions. Aversive thinking and aversive speaking are still possible; though I would advise anyone who proposed to speak out against the invasions of Afghanistan and Iraq to take the precaution of being already famous and therefore beyond the reach of the attorney general's arm. Noam Chomsky, George Soros, Edward Kennedy, Howard Dean, Paul Krugman, Sean Penn, and Maureen Dowd are unlikely to be arrested under the Patriot Act, but less visible critics, such as the editors of *Mother Jones,* have no reason to think themselves secure.

5

What has this to do with Emerson? A lot, in fact. Over the past ten or fifteen years a fairly systematic attempt has been made to recruit Emerson to the cause of Pragmatism. It is now widely claimed that America has a valid philosophic tradition extending from Emerson through William James, C. S. Peirce, John Dewey, G. H. Mead, and Santayana (if we allow him to be for this purpose an American), to Kenneth Burke and Richard Rorty. If this is a viable tradition, and has as its chief merit its practical relation to the world, then it can be invoked to sustain a corresponding politics, including American ambitions of power and empire. It seems to me that the tradition is a method, not a philosophy: it has nothing to say of first and last things, and it takes pride in having nothing to say about them. As a method, it is a theory of language. Hilary Putnam has argued, persuasively in my view, that Pragmatism is merely a bad theory:

> About a century ago, Charles Sanders Peirce asserted that the meaning of an "intellectual conception" is identical with the "sum" of its "practical consequences." And he thought this idea sufficiently important that he made it the primary maxim of the philosophy he called Pragmatism. This is nothing but an early statement of the Verifiability Theory of Meaning. And Pragmatism was the first philosophy dedicated to the proposition that

> theory of meaning can solve or dissolve the traditional problems of philosophy.
>
> Today the Verifiability Theory of Meaning has been pretty well abandoned, not, alas! because the fundamental intuition behind it has been universally conceded to be erroneous, but simply because there are formidable *technical* objections to the doctrine.[36]

By contrast with this prosaic method, European philosophy is alleged to be hopelessly pretentious, garrulous to no end. Pragmatists claim to take one step at a time and to gain efficacy by setting aside the ultimate questions of life and death. Richard Rorty wants philosophy to give up the metaphysical ghost and turn itself into politics. It would be an immense boon to the tradition if Emerson could be designated its origin, and his resignation from the Unitarian ministry in 1832 deemed to be the founding act of an indigenous philosophy, secular, American in every respect, cut loose from the religious preoccupations of Cotton Mather and Jonathan Edwards.

Cavell's position on this attempt to recruit Emerson to Pragmatism is interesting. He has for many years protested that American culture has repressed Emerson and Thoreau; that is, refused to acknowledge them as philosophers at all, preferring to regard them as personages, eccentrics, sages, mere writers, poets. Cavell regards them as philosophers, their writings worth as much thought, and the same kind of thought, as the writings of Kant,

Hegel, and Nietzsche. But he is not willing to have Emerson and his version of Transcendentalism subsumed in the prehistory of Pragmatism. He wants them to be thought of in a complex relation to Plato, Descartes, Kant, Nietzsche, Heidegger, and Wittgenstein. How otherwise could they be taken seriously as philosophers? The proposed assimilation of Emerson to Pragmatism, according to Cavell, "unfailingly blunts the particularity, the achievement, of Emerson's language." He also maintains that what calls for thinking in Emerson "occurs before—or as—our life of perplexities and aspirations and depressions and desperations and manifestations of destiny resolve themselves into practical problems."[37] That is: resolve themselves into the kind of problems a Pragmatist would want to address.

I have been describing the attempt to bring Emerson into American society. But if you bring him in, you find that your guest is not Emerson but James Russell Lowell. Emerson is a fearsome person because he claims the power of creating himself, becoming God to himself, and the fact that he makes the same claim for everyone does not take the harm out of it. If you stand thrilled by the sight of Emerson creating himself, you call him a strong poet, as Harold Bloom does. If you are appalled by the pretension and think it satanic, you know why America has repressed Emerson or domesticated him. He sets terrible conditions for his being willing to be human. The first of these is that he must be divine. The other conditions follow from that one.

The most telling parable of "the personalist authenticity of Emerson and the Emersonians"—it is Geoffrey Hill's phrase[38]—is (so far as my reading goes) Lawrence Sargent Hall's short story "The Ledge," written in 1959. A fisherman goes out on Christmas Day with his son, aged thirteen, and his nephew, aged fifteen, to hunt sea ducks along the outer ledges of the bay. He is a hard, fierce man, master of himself. He is the sort of man who might have said, as President Bush belatedly did, "Let's roll." But he is also capable of being driven to affection and tenderness. The fisherman and the boys start up the skiff with an outboard engine and transfer it to the big boat, anchored farther out, securing it on the stern. "From the mouth of the channel he could lay a straight course for Brown Cow Island, anchor the boat out of sight behind it, and from the skiff set their tollers off Devil's Hump three hundred yards to seaward." It takes them two hours at full throttle to reach the Hump. When they come to it, they anchor the big boat, take the skiff—loaded with their guns, knapsacks, and tollers—to the ledge and set the decoys. When the first flock of ducks comes over, the hunters shoot into them. Then the fisherman and his son take the skiff to gather up the dead birds. They return to the ledge and pull the skiff up to wait for the next flight of ducks. When they prepare to head for home, they find that the skiff has drifted away and is now a quarter of a mile to leeward. For a moment, the fisherman considers trying to swim for it, but it is impossible. "He simply sat down on the ledge and forgot everything except the marvelous mystery." The mystery is presumably what you divine when, like the fisherman in this predicament, you are for a moment or two beyond good and evil. The hunters try to attract attention by firing off their guns. The tide is rising, covering the ledge. In the event, and inevitably, the fisherman and the boys are drowned. The story ends with these sentences:

> As the land mass pivoted toward sunlight the day after Christmas, a tiny fleet of small craft converged off shore like iron filings to a magnet. At daybreak they found the skiff floating unscathed off the headland, half full of ducks and snow. The shooting *had* been good, as someone hearing on the mainland the previous afternoon had supposed. Two hours afterward they found the unharmed boat adrift five miles at sea. At high noon they found the fisherman at ebb tide, his right foot jammed cruelly into a glacial crevice of the ledge beside three shotguns, his hands tangled behind him in his suspenders, and under his right elbow a rubber boot with a sock and a live starfish in it. After dragging unlit depths all day for the boys, they towed the fisherman home in his own boat at sundown, and in the frost of evening, mute with discovering purgatory, laid him on his wharf for his wife to see.
>
> She, somehow, standing on the dock as in her frequent dream, gazing at the fisherman pure as crystal on the icy boards, a small rubber boot still frozen under one

> clenched arm, saw him exaggerated beyond remorse or grief, absolved of his mortality.

I read this story as a parable, dire indeed, of Emersonian self-reliance. The fisherman, immersed in circumstantial forces, insists on creating himself despite those forces. Such a man has several possibilities. If he is lucky, he can win, surviving to have the gratification of being master of himself. If he is not lucky, he can assent to the conditions of his life, as the fisherman does when he tells his son that he could not swim out to the skiff. "'A hundred yards maybe, in this water. I wish I could,' he added. It was the most intimate and pitiful thing he had ever said."[39] Or, still without luck, he could drive himself beyond good and evil, as if he determined not to be willing to live. To live is to be among conditions, willingly if one is wise. In the end, the one who understands this last possibility and settles for it is the fisherman's wife, when she looks at the corpse on the dock; the fisherman "pure as crystal on the icy boards." She sees him "exaggerated beyond remorse or grief, absolved of his mortality." It is an Emersonian exaggeration, the American version of hubris. Absolved of his mortality: released, removed from its further claims.

2

Moby-Dick

in the slush
Of this old Quaker graveyard where the bones
Cry out in the long night for the hurt beast
Bobbing by Ahab's whaleboats in the East.

—Robert Lowell, "The Quaker Graveyard in Nantucket"

I

When we refer to literature and its contexts, we mean to advert to the various ways in which a particular work is sensitive to forces at large. Some of these are immitigably personal, an affiliation of genetic, familial, and social circumstances. Some are more distant: the forces, political, economic, religious, or cultural, by which a writer is surrounded and, it may be, beset. A writer may yield to any or all of these forces, or may press back against them. Some of them may be ignorable. Jane Austen paid little attention to current affairs. George Eliot seems to have ignored nothing. Joyce lived in Europe through one war and the start of another without letting his mind be deflected by news from the Front. There is a choice. When we speak of the contexts of reading, we allow for choices. Sometimes one takes up a book and withdraws into its privacy: the world outside might as well not exist. At other times, one is reading with half a mind and listening, with the other half, for a knock on the door. Sometimes not even half of one's mind is available, and the knock on the door brings demands that can't be ignored. The context of reading also includes the other people who have read the same book and made sense of it in ways that don't coincide with one's own. Ideally, reading is a conversation, a debate, a round table, a seminar. But the ideal conditions are hard to find. We create them notionally or in default.

In 1972 I gave the T. S. Eliot Memorial Lectures at the University of Kent at Canterbury under the title "The Prometheans." The title did not survive much scrutiny. While preparing the lectures for publication I changed it to *Thieves of Fire,* an allusion to Rimbaud's claim, in a letter of May 15, 1871, to Paul Demeny, that the poet is a thief of fire. In the lectures I tried to describe a certain type of imagination which I called Promethean or peremptory because it is dissatisfied with the available forms of language and tries to drive beyond them or refute them. Writers possessed of such an imagination want to dislodge the common forms in favor of their own personalities, as if those could be found only in violence before or after language. They are charismatics, if not heretics, in relation to the structures they are given. Mostly, they accept from the past only its trouble. To represent this type of imagination, I spoke mainly of Milton, Blake, Melville, and D. H. Lawrence.

I do not intend to recite what I said in Canterbury, but I should mention the assumptions I made in the lectures, and especially in the one on Melville, which dealt mainly with *Moby-Dick.* I started that lecture by adverting to one Promethean possibility, that the imagination would consort with a writer's exorbitant will and create not a monster separate from itself but a monstrous form of itself, such that two figures would seem to live violently together under a single name and in the same body. Do we not feel, when we read *Moby-Dick,* that Melville's imagination has incited itself to create a ghostly presence surrounding the visible body of Ahab, a second man created by the first in pride and rage until the second engulfs the first and nothing of the first remains but its belated testimony in other men? Ahab is distinguished from other men who have no shadows, no ghosts; they are first persons singular without ambiguity, they coincide with themselves. Starbuck is the most complete example of this at-oneness, and Bulkington is only less complete because at an early stage in the book he is removed from the scene. Where there is a shadow, as in Fedallah, it is because he is, as Yvor Winters pointed out, "some kind of emanation from Ahab himself."[1] Melville makes this clear in chapter 73, where Stubb and Flask have been talking of Fedallah as Beelzebub: "Meantime, Fedallah was calmly eyeing the right whale's head, and ever and anon glancing from the deep wrinkles there to the lines in his own hand. And Ahab chanced so to stand, that the Parsee occupied his shadow; while, if the Parsee's shadow was there at all it seemed only to blend with, and lengthen Ahab's."[2]

In Fedallah, as C. L. R. James says, "Ahab sees his forethrown shadow; in Ahab Fedallah sees his abandoned substance."[3]

My intention in the Eliot Memorial Lectures was entirely or merely descriptive. I recognized a particular type of imagination and thought it could be distinguished from other types, as Milton's differed from George Herbert's not only in scale and reach but in the direction of its force. I felt no misgiving about using the vocabulary of imagination and genius. I did not believe that such words had been invalidated by any acts of literary theory, or that to speak of Melville's imagination was to fall into mystification and drive discourse beyond the reach of syntax. So far as I had a working theory of reading, it was a simple one: I was persuaded that the main value of a work of literature is that it stirs me to imagine forms of life different from my own, and by so doing helps me to convert into consciousness what would otherwise be the sundry of my life. I believed not that literature would redeem me but that it would help me to enlarge my range of apprehension and sympathy. So in reading *Moby-Dick* I made much of those passages in which Melville imagines the doubling or double being I tried to describe; as in chapter 44, "The Chart," where Ahab is penciling additional lines on a map to indicate where whales had been caught or seen on voyages by other ships. Melville writes:

> While thus employed, the heavy pewter lamp suspended in chains over his head, continually rocked with the motion of the ship, and for ever threw shifting gleams and

> shadows of lines upon his wrinkled brow, till it almost seemed that while he himself was marking out lines and courses on the wrinkled charts, some invisible pencil was also tracing lines and courses upon the deeply marked chart of his forehead.

Melville's move from literal lines to figurative, from a visible to an invisible pencil, is repeated in more extreme terms later in the chapter when Ahab rushes from his cabin "as though escaping from a bed that was on fire." Melville imagines that the Ahab who penciled the map and the Ahab who rushed from his cabin were not one and the same:

> For, at such times, crazy Ahab, the scheming, unappeasedly steadfast hunter of the white whale; this Ahab that had gone to his hammock, was not the agent that so caused him to burst from it in horror again. The latter was the eternal, living principle or soul in him; and in sleep, being for the time dissociated from the characterizing mind, which at other times employed it for its outer vehicle or agent, it spontaneously sought escape from the scorching contiguity of the frantic thing, of which, for the time, it was no longer an integral. But as the mind does not exist unless leagued with the soul, therefore it must have been that, in Ahab's case, yielding up all his thoughts and fancies to his one supreme purpose; that purpose, by its own sheer inveteracy of will,

> forced itself against gods and devils into a kind of self-assumed, independent being of its own. Nay, could grimly live and burn, while the common vitality to which it was conjoined, fled horror-stricken from the unbidden and unfathered birth. Therefore, the tormented spirit that glared out of bodily eyes, when what seemed Ahab rushed from his room, was for the time but a vacated thing, a formless somnambulistic being, a ray of living light, to be sure, but without an object to color, and therefore a blankness in itself. God help thee, old man, thy thoughts have created a creature in thee; and he whose intense thinking thus makes him a Prometheus; a vulture feeds upon that heart for ever; that vulture the very creature he creates.[4]

The style is not pellucid, it sends us lurching from one opaque word to the next without letting us divine what these words mean: agent, principle, soul, mind, being, vitality, and spirit. Melville is forcing sentences to do more than sentences equably can. We respond to the demand in the words more clearly than to the words. A mild paraphrase would have it that in Ahab, soul and mind—in other people normally at one—were dissociated from each other. Soul tried to escape from mind, and mind, identified with Ahab's supreme purpose, took on a kind of independent being. As such, it lived by its own fire, while the body fled horror-stricken from the unbidden and unfathered birth. What rushed out, in

C. L. R. James's terms, was "the common humanity flying from the monster that had overcome it."[5] Ahab is Prometheus, except that he has created his own punishment, the vulture that feeds on his heart.

I chose those and other passages from *Moby-Dick* not in the hope of giving a comprehensive account of the book but to illustrate what I regarded as the particular bias or prejudice of Melville's imagination. I thought of the Promethean imagination as a continuous possibility. It would appear in different writers, like a family resemblance consistent with differences in detail and profile. I did not think it necessary to reflect on the social, political, and religious forces at large that might at a particular time thwart the imagination and at other times might enable its processes. Nor did I concern myself with the mobility or moodiness of a reader who might read *Paradise Lost, Women in Love, Moby-Dick,* or Blake's *Milton* in one way today and differently tomorrow. I am not confessing to sins on my part in referring to these assumptions: they were devices of economy at the time, and they still seem to me valid though not blithely or self-evidently so. But the passing of thirty years has made many differences.

2

As a student at University College, Dublin, I grew up into the reading of literature under the sway of the New Criticism, which I thought of as founded on Coleridge and Eliot and stretching its wings in the work of I. A. Richards, William Empson, John

Crowe Ransom, F. R. Leavis, Cleanth Brooks, R. P. Blackmur, Yvor Winters, and Kenneth Burke. These critics did not constitute a school, but they acknowledged a vague kinship of interests. I felt their influence mostly in the reading of poems. Richards and Brooks presented poems as "well-wrought urns" in which conflicting impulses were eventually resolved, reconciled as an achieved form. The force of reconciliation might be called genius—though not in Emerson's more universal sense—meaning presence of mind to a supreme degree. Burke elucidated Keats's "Ode on a Grecian Urn" and other poems and fictions as "symbolic actions." Blackmur was attentive to moments in poems in which language seems to intuit "the sublime" beyond concept or argument. Novels were more difficult to manage, they were too long to be controlled by a single act of attention, and in some cases—Dostoevsky and Tolstoy, for instance—there were problems of translation which thwarted an analysis of the language. So I tended to look more variously for guidance on fiction—to Henry James, Erich Auerbach, E. M. Forster, Allen Tate, and Mark Schorer, I recall. I don't recall when I first read *Moby-Dick*, "Billy Budd," and "Bartleby the Scrivener." I knew that the reception of *Moby-Dick* since its publication in 1851 was a confused story and that the process of making the book canonical did not begin until a year or two before 1919, the centenary of Melville's birth. Starting with Carl Van Doren's essay in 1917 and Raymond Weaver's two years later, nearly every major critic felt impelled to intervene. Lawrence's *Studies in Classic American Literature* was published in

1923, but when I came to read it, I thought it too exalted to be locally useful. I considered it significant that in 1938 Blackmur wrote an essay, "The Craft of Herman Melville," and in the same year Yvor Winters included a long chapter on Melville in *Maule's Curse.* I don't think I realized, when I read Blackmur's essay several years later, that he had bewildered himself by bringing to bear on *Moby-Dick* and *Pierre* critical principles derived from Henry James, principles—cogent in themselves and in their bearing on the history of fiction—that were bound to be frustrated by the errancy of Melville's narrative procedures. Melville did not seem to care about composition, the legality of the privileged point of view, the primacy of consciousness, or—in any clear understanding of them—the claims of form. No wonder Blackmur thought Melville's only working principle a process of vagary: he was hardly a novelist at all, at least in the sense in which Stendhal, Flaubert, James, and Joyce were novelists. Winters was much more accommodating toward *Moby-Dick* than Blackmur was, mainly because he was not perturbed by the mixture of the professional discourse of whaling with the narrative and descriptive chapters.

At that time, while some of us took our bearings from the New Critics, the general sense of American literature that obtained in Europe after the war was the one expressed in F. O. Matthiessen's *American Renaissance: Art and Experience in the Age of Emerson and Whitman* (1941). There were other books, closer to home in Dublin: the most influential of those was Marcus Cunliffe's *The Literature of the United States* (1954), which pronounced on American literature, like a severe headmaster: "has made progress, but could do better." Cunliffe saved us from being entirely dependent on Henry Nash Smith, Leo Marx, Perry Miller, and Roy Harvey Pearce. But *American Renaissance* was more authoritative than Cunliffe's book. Matthiessen wrote the book, starting to work on it in the early thirties, to make a claim for American culture as an operative force to be set against the threat that culminated in the rise of Nazism and Fascism. He was a strong cultural scholar, but not a disinterested or aesthetic reader. In *American Renaissance* he started from the glowing fact that American culture produced, within a space of five years, Emerson's *Representative Men* (1850), Hawthorne's *The Scarlet Letter* (1850) and *The House of the Seven Gables* (1851), Melville's *Moby-Dick* (1851), Thoreau's *Walden* (1854), and Whitman's *Leaves of Grass* (1855). That was enough to justify Matthiessen's speaking of an American renaissance. So far as I know, nobody questioned the claim until Perry Miller published *Nation's Nation* (1967) and argued that "Hawthorne and Melville do not inaugurate a 'renaissance' in American literature; they constitute a culmination, they pronounce a funeral oration on the dreams of their youth, they intone an elegy of disenchantment." Miller's center of gravity was the New England mind of the seventeenth century, so he was bound to read the movement from Jonathan Edwards to Emerson as a relaxation of tension, a diminished scale of belief and concern. He also adverted to the fact that Hawthorne and Melville "were crushed before the juggernaut of the novel," the popular middle-brow or low-brow novel, such as Charles Fenno Hoffman's *Greyslaer* (1840) that went through edition after edition.[6]

Matthiessen interpreted *Moby-Dick* as a conflict not essentially between Ahab and the white whale but between Ahab and Ishmael. Ahab represented totalitarianism, but he started out as a distinctive American aberration, Emerson gone wrong. Ishmael was a type of American democracy, as his dealings with Queequeg and the crew of the *Pequod* made clear. Ahab's tragedy "is that of an unregenerate will, which stifles his soul and drives his brain with an inescapable fierceness." He is an inadequate tragic hero: he suffers, but he is not transformed by his suffering:

> Melville created in Ahab's tragedy a fearful symbol of the self-enclosed individualism that, carried to its furthest extreme, brings disaster both upon itself and upon the group of which it is a part. He provided also an ominous glimpse of what was to result when the Emersonian will to virtue became in less innocent natures the will to power and conquest.

Ahab's career "is prophetic of many others in the history of later nineteenth-century America":

> Man's confidence in his own unaided resources has seldom been carried farther than during that era in this country. The strong-willed individuals who seized the land and gutted the forests and built the railroads were

> no longer troubled with Ahab's obsessive sense of evil, since theology had receded even farther into their backgrounds. But their drives were as relentless as his, and they were to prove like him in many other ways also, as they went on to become the empire builders of the post–Civil War world. They tended to be as dead to enjoyment as he, as blind to everything but their one pursuit, as unmoved by fear or sympathy, as confident in assuming an identification of their wills with immutable plan or manifest destiny, as liable to regard other men as merely arms and legs for the fulfillment of their purposes, and, finally, as arid and exhausted in their burnt-out souls.[7]

Ahab's sultanism drives him to destroy ship, crew, and ultimately himself. Ishmael survives to tell the tale and to make sense of the catastrophe. His survival proves, in Matthiessen's version, the paramount value of American literary and intellectual culture since the years of Emerson, Whitman, Hawthorne, Melville, and Thoreau.

It is not surprising that Matthiessen's book became the authoritative guide to the development of American studies in Europe after 1945, a project that soon became a small part of the rhetoric of the Cold War. Matthiessen's values were nearly as European as they were American, a commitment he showed in his books on Henry James and on T. S. Eliot. And while he was in his political convictions a man of the Left and was widely regarded in America as a fellow traveler, he largely kept international politics out of *American Renaissance*—another feature that made it attractive to Europeans who had not yet begun to think of the United States as an imperial power and preferred to construe politics in the more tractable form of literary culture. Not that Matthiessen's sensibility was as coherent as it appeared. In *American Renaissance* he suppressed every objection he felt toward American culture for the sake of the "war effort." After the war, he joined with Alfred Kazin, Margaret Mead, Wassily Leontiev, and other scholars to teach at the Salzburg Seminar in American Studies, and he extended his tour of cultural duty to include some weeks at the Charles University in Prague. The memoir he published of those months before the coup in Czechoslovakia in 1948—*From the Heart of Europe*—is much more critical of American culture than he allowed himself to be in *American Renaissance.* But he continued to speak of Ahab's "indomitable will." "The single individual, a law only to himself, treats his entire crew as mere appendages to his own ruthless purpose, and sweeps them all finally to destruction." "No more challenging counterstatement to Emerson's self-reliance," Matthiessen said, "has yet been written."[8]

American Renaissance established the force of orthodoxy for its time, and largely governed the direction of American studies in the work of Lionel Trilling, Richard Chase, Richard Sewall, Charles Feidelson, Marius Bewley, and other scholars. Even when they disagreed with Matthiessen, their disagreement was a nuance of his sense of American culture. Bewley, for instance, argued that Ahab represents "the transition . . . between the American democratic acceptance of creation, and hatred of that creation." The essential conflict in *Moby-Dick* is between Ahab's attitude toward the white whale and Ishmael's. Ishmael's is one of "respectful reverence and wonder"; to him the whale is not a symbol of evil but "a magnificent symbol of creation itself." Ahab proceeds with dreadful righteousness from his severed limb "to a condemned and guilty universe," the white whale its assailable sign. Leviathan, especially in its greatest role of the whale, affirms everything that Ahab denies.[9]

Those of us who were involved in American studies in Europe after the war learned from Matthiessen, more than from anyone else, what we should think about the major books and the culture that produced them. We didn't know that we were implicated, however marginally, in the propaganda of the Cold War. Nor did we spend any time telling one another that the United States, in addition to using the atomic bomb and storing arsenals of weaponry of mass destruction—chemical, biological, and of every other kind—had culture high and popular, literature, dance, great orchestras, superb jazz, architecture, and painting. I didn't advert to the question of propaganda till April 1975, when Andrew Sinclair stormed out of a lecture being given by Gordon Wood in the Great Hall of the Schloss Leopoldskron in Salzburg. Sinclair protested against Wood's "sad and terrible words" and called the lecture—or as much of it as he had listened to—"a travesty." It didn't occur to me that Matthiessen's book, however extended in its implications, had anything to do with the American incursion into Vietnam. It seemed innocent to me. But the book has come in for a great deal of rebuke since 1941. Matthiessen is regularly accused of having turned *Moby-Dick* and other classic books into Cold War texts. The reason is that the moral lesson to be drawn from such books in 1941, as Matthiessen interpreted them, was still available when the common enemy, after the defeat of Nazism and Fascism, was deemed to be the Soviet Union, and the good cause of freedom was understood to be in the hands of the United States. After 1945, only the names had to be changed. In the past few years the rebuke against Matthiessen has been delivered mainly by Donald E. Pease, Jonathan Arac, and their colleagues among the New Americanists. I'll refer mainly to Pease.

3

Pease argues that the rhetorical strategies of the Cold War, by presenting the entire world as an opposition between the United States and the Soviet Union, cast all conflicts, in any part of the world, in terms of this opposition:

> So inclusive is this frame and so pervasive is its control of the interpretation of world events that there appear to be no alternatives to it. . . . In positing the conclusion rather than arriving at it through argument, the Cold War scenario produces as implicit the resolution that

> never has to become explicit. And in translating explicit political argument into the implicit resolution of that argument, the Cold War scenario silences dissent as effectively as did Ahab in the quarterdeck scene.

The bearing of this upon *Moby-Dick* is that "the scenes of cultural persuasion generated by the Cold War and Captain Ahab depend upon a radical form of displacement—one in which the specific terms of conflict or dissent are recast in other terms and on another scene." As in the quarterdeck episode, chapter 36. Pease remarks:

> Captain Ahab, when confronted with Starbuck's commonsense argument against his revenge quest, converts the commonsense opposition into a scenario in which Ahab's belief in his right to utter self-reliance has been violated by cosmic design. . . . Ahab's oratory elevates that contradiction into an ideal, revolutionary opposition between a free Ahab and a tyrannical universe.

Where Matthiessen kept Ahab and Ishmael separate, as principles in conflict, like Athens and Sparta, Pease brings them together as "a single self-conflicted will." Ishmael is just as obsessive as Ahab, though the obsessions are different and have different social correlations:

> In Ahab Melville condemned the self-interest at work in the oratory of the nation's politicians. In Ishmael he con-

> demned the cultural despair at work in the counter-rhetoric of the nation's transcendentalists. Ishmael and Ahab share not a visionary compact but a social contract in which each agreed to justify the other's self-interest.

Pease doesn't quite say that, as between Ahab and Ishmael, it's six of one and half a dozen of the other. He would agree, I assume, that the social type embodied in Ahab is at least immediately more dangerous than Ishmael's type; though in the long run the differences between them may be slight. According to Pease, Ahab tries to "provide a basis in the human will for a rhetoric that has lost all other sanction." He tries "to turn the coercion at work in his rhetoric into fate, a principle of order in a universe without it." But since his will "is grounded in the sense of loss, it is fated to perfect that loss in an act of total destruction." But Ishmael is also perverse, if not yet a catastrophe:

> Like Emerson, Ishmael uncouples the actions that occur from the motives giving rise to them, thereby turning all events in the narrative into an opportunity to display the powers of eloquence capable of taking possession of them. Indeed, nothing and no one resist Ishmael's power to convert the world that he sees into the forms of rhetoric that he wants. The question remains, however, whether Ishmael, in his need to convert all the facts in his world and all the events in his life into a persuasive power

> capable of recoining them as the money of his mind, is possessed of a will any less totalizing than Ahab's.

Pease forces the question to a hard conclusion. He speaks of Ishmael's will "moving from one intellectual model to another," seizing each, investing it "with the subjunctive power of his personality," and then, "in a display of restlessness no eloquence can arrest," turning to the next model as if each existed "only for this ever-unsatisfied movement of attention." Ishmael turns from one "as if" to another. And Pease asks: "Is such a will any less totalitarian, however indeterminate its local exertions, than a will to convert all the world into a single struggle"?[10] It begins to appear, though Pease doesn't say this, that Ishmael is a sophist, one of those who—as E. M. Cioran says, "having ceased to be *nature* live as a function of the word." Sophists are not oppressed by facts, because they know that "reality depends on the signs which express it and which must simply be mastered."[11] Not mastered once for all, but for the time being and until the next occasion arises. It is hard to say whether this applies more to Ishmael than to Melville as omniscient author. The first words of the book indicate that it is Ishmael's story, and that he has survived every catastrophe to tell it; but then for many chapters he disappears and the voice we hear is Melville's rather than Ishmael's. Ishmael is less a character than the trajectory of one style displaced by another and yet another. So much so, that it is hard to be convinced that he has any personal identity or "that there is anything to his saying 'I.'"[12] Not that this would undermine Ishmael's force in the book, if what is required is an omnivorous or a promiscuous rhetoric; but it would emphasize that he is only nominally a character to be described in terms of a totalitarian will. He is rather a force of presence—totalitarian, indeed—among the words. He cannot embody the redemptive character of American culture, as Matthiessen claimed.

The genre that enforces the Cold War scenario, according to Pease, is the romance. Interpretations within the field of American studies sought "to dissolve the contradictory relations between the nation and the state." The idea of the nation continued to thrive on notions of "manifest destiny" and "Exceptionalism," but the state as distinct from the nation needed a genre to enforce itself; it had to be at one with a geopolitical fantasy:

> The imagined domestic community through which the state conducted its policy of Americanization at home and abroad depended on the romance genre for the emplotment of its fantasy. The fantasy involved controlling the globe's ideological map. It was underwritten by an interpretive method produced within the field of American Literary Studies known as the myth-symbol school. The method derived its authority from endowing its practitioners with the capacity to represent entire cultures as ritual reenactments of this national fantasy. It yoked an anthropological imaginary to ritualistic ex-

> plications of others' cultural stories and facilitated exchanges between literary and geopolitical realms that effectively transformed the field of American Studies into an agency of neocolonialism. Its practitioners designed a cultural typology with which to interpret and thereafter to subsume other literatures and geopolitical spaces into a universal Americanism.[13]

The moral of the romance would always be the same. Prospero must turn out to be an American, and to impose American values on everyone from Caliban to Ferdinand. Those who adopted the vocabulary of myth and symbol hoped to present experience in grand principles without paying much attention to local details and differences.

Pease wants to disable the Cold War scenario, as he calls it, by removing the allegory that he thinks made it possible. But he has not recognized that allegory and romance issue from different motives. Romance is not obedient to "the schematic one-for-one correspondences of allegory," as Donald Davie calls them in an essay in which he argues that myth and allegory are also "essentially different."[14] There is good reason to keep these terms separate. The allegory in *Moby-Dick* has always been a problem. Blackmur thought that its use nearly defeated the book. He argued that genuine allegory, as in *Pilgrim's Progress,* requires "the preliminary possession of a complete and stable body of belief appropriate to the theme in hand." Melville had no such belief;

neither had Hawthorne; nor anyone else in nineteenth-century America or since:

> Melville wrote Allegory in all the machinery of capital letter in the hope of finding—or creating—an absolute structure within which he could make a concert of the contrary powers of heaven and earth. Like Shakespeare, he had to make a concord out of discord, and especially out of the shifting discords of good and evil. His story could never be content to be a story, or its own meaning, but was compelled to assert a meaning which had not yet come to pass.[15]

Melville could not have practiced allegory to good purpose, if only because of "the peculiarly confused, inconsistent and incomplete state of belief he was in." In the craft of writing, Blackmur maintains, "artificial allegory, like willed mysticism (of which Melville showed a trace), is a direct and easy mode only in that it puts so much in by intention as to leave nearly everything out in execution." In the event, Melville's allegory in *Moby-Dick* kept breaking down, and "with each resumption got more and more verbal, and more and more at the mercy of the encroaching event it was meant to transcend."[16]

Blackmur insists on the necessity, in an allegorical writer as in his readers, of a complete and stable body of belief, and he thinks that for the purposes of allegory nothing less would do. But there are writers who thrive on less. Allen Tate claimed that Emily

Dickinson derived certain advantages from the general condition of belief, such as it was, in New England and from the unmoored nature of her own belief. She was native to the Puritan heritage she did not profess, and she lived on moods of yes, no, and maybe. As a consequence, she had an experimental relation to belief rather than the secure or even the doubtful possession of it. This may have resulted in inadequacies of various kinds, but Dickinson's imagination was such that she needed experiment, confusion, doubt, blasphemy, and the intermittences of faith and despair as another writer needs a settled conviction or an unassailable atheism. It is true that she did not practice allegory as Melville did, and maybe that invalidates the comparison. I offer it merely to say that one writer may do as well with a quizzical relation to her tradition as another with a devout grasp of it.

Winters differed from Blackmur on Melville. He regarded Melville and his readers as still having enough Calvinism in them to make the allegory feasible. Pease reminds us that "allegory is a literary form with origins in a community rather than a private person."[17] But a community may hold together sufficiently for most purposes on shreds and patches of a remembered code. Winters thinks that Melville could count on more determinant values. He remarks that while the Nantucket sea officers are nominally Quakers, they "have more of the Calvinist in their make-up than of the Friend, and Melville treats them in more or less Calvinistic terms; they are, says Melville, 'Quakers with a vengeance.'" As a result, according to Winters, Melville can present

Ahab as a man in a state of sin: "His sin, in the minor sense, is monomaniac vengeance; in the major, the will to destroy the spirit of evil itself, an intention blasphemous because beyond human powers and infringing upon the purposes of God." The sin is made worse, Winters believes, not only by Ahab's determination on vengeance but by his conviction "that a power greater and more malignant than any proper to mere animal nature is acting in or through the whale."[18] Ahab is convinced of "the demonism of the world," a phrase we read in chapter 42, "The Whiteness of the Whale."

Unless you want to get rid of the allegory, Winters seems to me to make a strong case for a Calvinist sense of it. But the Calvinist emphasis has an immense disadvantage: it nearly prevents us from registering Melville's conviction of the categorical interpenetration of good and evil. He seems not to have believed that they could be separated as moral principles without obscuring the human nature the separation offers to clarify. It is the indigence of language that makes us think the separation, stark indeed, is valid. In *Moby-Dick* ambergris, the sweetest-smelling substance, is found in the bowels of a blighted whale. Ishmael is saved by Queequeg's coffin. Pease wants to get rid of the allegory in *Moby-Dick,* but not because it keeps us blind to Melville's sense of the ambiguity in life, or the incorrigible confounding of what we take as principles. It is reason enough for him that allegory, like the other devices with which he links it—fantasy, romance, myth, symbol—maintains the Cold War agenda as a structure of implicitly aggressive motives. Allegory identifies the world with the American fantasy of it. My own sense of the matter is that these devices are desperate measures: they are what you practice when (in Blackmur's terms) the only story you have to tell asserts a meaning that has not yet come to pass.

But even in the Cold War scenario there are difficulties. To make it hold, you have to keep the conflict, as Matthiessen did, between Ahab and Ishmael. Starbuck's argument for common sense and duty is worthy, so far as it goes, but it has no chance against Ahab's will, and in the end Starbuck yields to the stronger force. Then there is the white whale. The allegory, especially in Winters's version, needs a principle of some kind, having Manichaean or other force sinister enough to drive Ahab mad. Northrop Frye took the sea in *Moby-Dick* to be "an element of alienation," and the white whale as presumably the supreme manifestation of that. The obsession in Ahab keeps driving him into alienation, "so that he in a sense loves what he hates."[19] Other readers have taken the whale as Ahab's projection of himself. It may be that these anthropological and psychological readings are designed to escape from the political reading and its acrimony. But the book is diminished if you don't take the whale seriously or if you regard it as a mere excuse for human excesses. You hardly need the whale at all if, with C. L. R. James, you consider Ahab "the most dangerous and destructive social type that has ever appeared in Western Civilization."[20] By calling Ahab the totalitarian personality, you interpret the *Pequod* as modern industrial or postindustrial civilization, and Fedallah as Ahab's shadow minion who runs the corporation and makes poor people poorer. Starbuck and everyone else fill their minor roles.

But a characteristic quality of Melville's language in *Moby-Dick* makes a further problem for allegory. Grant that Melville was committed to literature as representation. The elaborate account of the whaling industry is proof of that commitment, even though it is provisional. The business of whaling, as I argued in *Thieves of Fire,* stands for everything in the world that engages one's interest, subject to the qualification that it leaves one's most demanding interest famished: it is what one attends to, and rightly, but only for now, biding one's time, waiting for the real other thing.[21] Still, the urge to represent is genuine. Moby Dick is the name of a certain whale: we are asked to believe in its existence. It is only on the strength of that existence that *Moby-Dick* acquires the resonance of a myth, a story told for the benefit of the community to which it is addressed. The fact that American culture has never wanted to hear this story accounts for Melville's crazed insistence on telling it. For Melville, merely to exist (as whale or as person) is not enough. That there is no language for what he declares to exceed the whale's mere existence, or Ahab's, makes a problem for him and for us.

We may let the silent argument between Winters and Blackmur rest, and decide at our leisure whether the apparent allegorical intention is fulfilled or not. But whatever else an allegorist needs, he needs to be sure that he knows what he is talking about.

A writer who aspires to the sublime may dispense himself from this requirement: there aren't words for everything. Melville may have hoped that he could at once practice the observances of representation and allegory and, in the next breath, transcend those categories by projecting one unmoored *altitudo* after another. I'm not sure that readers have registered these excesses as sublime. Robert Martin Adams has commented on what he calls the "clogged allegory" of *Moby-Dick*. The allegory is clogged or perhaps defeated not by the fact that its meaning is not available in the society to which it is directed but by the fact that, as the styles of the book keep insisting, the meaning is so elusive as to be inexpressible. Melville, as Adams remarks, "is continually suggesting another order of experience, a totality which is not the sum of specific qualities, a dimension which is not the total of finite magnitudes."[22] Adams is thinking of those passages in which the whale is claimed to elude all categories. At various moments in the book we read of "one grand hooded phantom," we hear of "the undeliverable, nameless perils of the whale," its "outrageous strength with an inscrutable malice sinewing it," and every few pages we are admonished to think of "the heartless voids and immensities of the universe," "the ungraspable phantom of life," and "dim shuddering glimpses into Polar eternities." Like Adams, James Guetti claims that in *Moby-Dick* "the illusion of meaning remains." The "multiple and unresolved possibilities become—because they are unresolved—the supposed evidence of some unspeakable and immense consistency: they are evidence of the inexpressible, the image of something that is the greatest possible meaning because it is not meaning at all."[23] You may recall, and compare with Melville's rhetoric of inscrutability, F. R. Leavis's comment on Conrad's style in *Heart of Darkness:*

> Conrad must here stand convicted of borrowing the arts of the magazine-writer (who has borrowed his, shall we say, from Kipling and Poe) in order to impose upon his readers and on himself, for thrilled response, a "significance" that is merely an emotional insistence on the presence of what he can't produce. The insistence betrays the absence, the willed "intensity" the nullity. He is intent on making a virtue out of not knowing what he means.[24]

Leavis regards Conrad's rhetoric of inscrutability as a serious flaw in a great writer. Adams is impatient with it in Melville. He thinks *Moby-Dick* "a vast, reverberant shell of a book" in which "inadequacy of strenuous expression is offered as evidence for magnitude of conception." The book is "the triumph of an illusion and suggestion." The details—the struggling bird nailed to the sinking masthead, the coffin bursting from the vortex, the orphan-searching *Rachel*—these are "the mere dumb-show of allegory." But Adams at least glances at an interpretation of the book according to which its failure becomes its success: "For the antagonism between the eagerly grasping mind and elusive reality is fundamental to all other antagonisms in the book; so that it is the book's ultimate failure after exhaustive efforts to express its theme which is presumed to constitute best evidence of its success in handling it."[25] We recognize the authority of that failure. It transforms aesthetic or expressive limitation into moral triumph, grandeur, purity of heart; and it implies that a lesser artist than Melville would claim to know, with disgusting familiarity, the states of being he presumes to describe. Ahab and Ishmael are alike beyond syntax. Ahab insists that he can remove the dichotomy between mind and world by making the world part of himself. Ishmael lives among words on the only conviction available to him, that since truth is incommunicable, he can only move from one provisional rhetoric to another.

4

So how would I propose to read *Moby-Dick* now, now meaning since September 11, 2001, and the rise of George W. Bush as president and commander in chief? I start with the sad recognition that Bush has been remarkably successful in persuading the American people to endorse a simple allegory of good and evil. He has achieved this consensus not by reasoned argument but by taking it for granted. In 1938 Blackmur thought that the conditions of allegory were not present either in Melville or the readers he hoped to address. But Bush's allegory is so simple that most American people feel no misgiving in accepting it. They murmur "the war on terrorism" just as readily as he and Donald Rumsfeld do. This is strange. American culture takes it for granted that

Satan is dead. Evil does not exist, and where it seems to, it is explicable in terms of the evildoer's upbringing: an absent father, a broken family, a wretched environment. Charles Manson, Jeffrey Dahmer, and Timothy McVeigh are not evil, they simply had damaging early lives. Besides, these men are American citizens. Foreigners are given no such allowance. President Bush's "axis of evil" is a sinister fellowship of foreign countries. Osama bin Laden is evil, a simular man—to use an adjective of Emerson's when he thought of black men and Irish immigrants—men beneath the moral or spiritual level of what it means to be human. We—citizens or "resident aliens" of the United States—are good; unless we are of Arab or South Asian origin, in which case we can be labeled "unlawful enemy combatants" and arrested without trial and without counsel under the U.S. Patriot Act. They, the foreigners—being "terrorists" in the several countries accused of harboring them—are evil. (I put "terrorists" in quotation marks because many one-time terrorists are now international statesmen, as Saddam Hussein could still enjoy the support of the United States if he hadn't misinterpreted diplomatic signals from Washington and committed the excess of invading Kuwait.) We are good because we are dedicated to individual freedom and have always been exempt from the corruptions of feudalism and its European institutions.

It would be difficult, in these lurid circumstances, to read *Moby-Dick* as anything but a revenge play, a Jacobean melodrama of good and evil. As in *The Duchess of Malfi* and *The White Devil,* we find the range of feeling reduced to a few grandiose emotions, and these intensified to make a supreme claim upon our attention. Melodrama, not tragedy—no formal consolation or transcendence is available. The "spirit of the age" is one of retaliation, spontaneous certitude, there is no concession to what Whitman called "the curious whether and how." It is the Cold War all over again, except that the Soviet Union no longer exists and Evil is deemed for the moment to be the composite force of Muslim fundamentalism and the fanaticism it incites. The chances of success in killing every terrorist who has the destruction of American society and culture in mind are obviously poor—it is hardly possible, even for the United States, to bomb the sixty-six countries in which members of Al Qaeda are supposed to be operating—but President Bush and his cabinet are determined to carry forward in that cause a war without end. Most Americans seem to have accepted this New Cold War scenario now that it has become, in acceptably far-off countries, a Hot War. High-altitude bombing has ensured that only a few American soldiers (few by comparison with the numbers of Afghans and Iraqis) have been killed. In Afghanistan, eight thousand Afghans, according to the *New York Times,* have been killed, and far fewer Americans. The numbers of those killed in Iraq are not yet complete—there are killings, day by day—but dead Iraqis outnumber dead Americans, British, and other "Coalition" soldiers and "contractors." The mess in Iraq has not yet caused much consternation in the United States. At least for the time being, the spirit of revenge appears to be dominant: most Americans evidently approve the war, even though the justification given by Bush for going to war has turned out to be specious. Not that Ahab is to be identified with the president, his cabinet, and his advisers. In an allegorical reading of the book, they would correspond to Ahab, Starbuck, Ishmael, the *Pequod* and its crew, everyone determined to kill the white whale. In *Moby-Dick*, according to Donald Pease's reading, Ahab took the white whale as excuse for setting aside the contractual agreement he made with owners and crew to gather oil for the Nantucket market. The whale embodied cosmic malice sufficient to justify Ahab's rejecting the prosaic duty of collecting oil. Since September 11, then, the formally undeclared war against "terror" has proceeded, though such a war can't ever be won. America remains vulnerable to sporadic attacks, but the existence of a common enemy is supposed to keep the people united. The problems entailed in reconstituting Afghanistan and Iraq persist, but these are "in another country."

I am not immune to this rhetoric. I was in New York on September 11, 2001, and was as appalled as anyone else by the attacks on the World Trade Center and the Pentagon. I wondered, as days passed, what response the Bush administration could honorably make. Economic sanctions, diplomatic acts, Periclean wisdom, Christian forgiveness—love your enemy, do good to those who hate you—seemed implausible, given the mood of the American people. Besides, the admonition in Matthew and Luke to "love your enemies" seems to refer only to private relations. I recently came upon the passage in *The Concept of the Political* in which Carl Schmitt insists on a distinction between private enemy and public enemy, in Latin between *inimicus* and *hostis:*

> The enemy is solely the *public* enemy, because everything that has a relationship to such a collectivity of men, particularly to a whole nation, becomes *public* by virtue of such a relationship. Never in the thousand-year struggle between Christians and Moslems did it occur to a Christian to surrender rather than defend Europe out of love toward the Saracens or Turks. The enemy in the political sense need not be hated personally, and in the private sphere only does it make sense to love one's enemy, that is, one's adversary.[26]

Still, I hoped for some response from the Bush administration other than the bombing of mostly innocent people. "Only the unforgivable can be forgiven," Jacques Derrida said two years before September 11, 2001.[27] Perhaps it might be possible for Bush to act from deeper values than the popular immediacies of revenge; or from more profound motives than those of statecraft. No sign of that. The Treaty of Versailles is now regarded as a disaster, its punitive force having issued mainly in the rise of militant nationalism in Germany and the emergence of Hitler. A few days after September 11, at a ceremony in the National Cathedral in Washington, D.C., the Protestant Archbishop said—in the presence of

Bush and other dignitaries—that "we must not become the evil we claim to destroy." That was worth thinking about, but it seemed to bring about no second thought in those who listened to the homily. The primitive motives were already in place.

Reading *Moby-Dick* again now, it seems inevitable that we take it as a revenge tragedy, with all the simplicities that that entails. It is also a book of the Old Testament rather than the New. It has no place for a Sermon on the Mount or for turning the other cheek. Ahab has his humanities, as Melville says. In chapter 125 he lodges the boy Pip in his own cabin: "Come! I feel prouder leading thee by thy black hand, than though I grasped an Emperor's!"[28] It is an allusion and a response to Lear's creaturely acknowledgment of the Fool in the storm of act III, scene iv: "In, boy; go first. You houseless poverty,—/Nay, get thee in." But it is an aberration. Within a few pages Ahab refuses to help the *Rachel* to search for its lost boat, and then we have the three days of the chase for the white whale. The revenge play ends as most such plays do, in death nearly universal. "And I only am escaped alone to tell thee." There is no place for "perhaps" or "if" or "but."

What to make of all this? We need an interpretation independent of the Americanization of politics and anthropology. We should release ourselves from the assumption that there is one story and one story only, and that it is an American story in fulfillment of America's manifest destiny. The reading of *Moby-Dick* should take a literary and, yes, aesthetic form, bearing in mind that aesthetics means perception and an aesthetic reading deems the book to be offered only to be perceived. There is no merit in replacing one allegory with another. We are reading a disparate book; parts of it are descriptions of the natural world, sermons, soliloquies, elucidations of the trade and appurtenances of whaling; parts allude to revenge tragedy, epic poetry, romances, yarns of the sea, adventure stories, Cervantes's Don Quixote, Milton's Satan, Shakespeare's Macbeth, Lear, and the Fool. Readers have not known how to read the white whale. In *Call Me Ishmael* Charles Olson interpreted it as "all the hidden forces that terrorise man,"—Death, for short.[29] Yvor Winters took the whale as "the chief symbol and spirit of evil."[30] James Wood, perhaps acknowledging the death of Satan, interprets the whale as God and Devil, a composite of forces perhaps equally lethal to man.[31] In *Thieves of Fire* I took the whale to be a symbol of limits, "the wall, the hard circumference of things, as well as everything contained in Robert Lowell's 'IS, the whited monster,' in 'The Quaker Graveyard in Nantucket': life itself, beyond which there is nothing, the void."[32] But what we need, in thinking of the whale, is not an allegory in which it may take its place but a more subtle figuring, on the lines of Frye's commentary in *Anatomy of Criticism,* where the theme is the heraldic symbol. I am aware of Pease's objection to the criticism that deals in myth and symbol, but this passage from Frye knows its limits and observes them:

> Still another is the kind of image described by Mr. Eliot as an objective correlative, the image that sets up an in-

> ward focus of emotion in poetry and at the same time substitutes itself for an idea. Still another, closely related to if not identical with the objective correlative, is the heraldic symbol, the central emblematic image which comes most readily to mind when we think of the word "symbol" in modern literature. We think, for example, of Hawthorne's scarlet letter, Melville's white whale, James's golden bowl, or Virginia Woolf's lighthouse. Such an image differs from the image of the formal allegory in that there is no continuous relationship between art and nature. In contrast to the allegorical symbols of Spenser, for instance, the heraldic emblematic image is in a paradoxical and ironic relation to both narrative and meaning. As a unit of meaning, it arrests the narrative; as a unit of narrative, it perplexes the meaning. It combines the qualities of Carlyle's intrinsic symbol with significance in itself, and the extrinsic symbol which points quizzically to something else.[33]

Frye's reference to "paradoxical and ironic relation" has the merit of preventing us from engaging in the simple conversion of the whale into a quasi-allegorical abstraction.

I value, too, Frye's description of *Moby-Dick* as a hybrid of romance and anatomy, "where the romantic theme of the wild hunt expands into an encyclopaedic anatomy of the whale."[34] And

Kenneth Burke's emphasis, in *A Grammar of Motives*, on Ahab and the dialectic of the scapegoat:

> When the attacker chooses for himself the object of attack, it is usually his blood brother; the debunker is much closer to the debunked than others are; Ahab was pursued by the white whale he was pursuing; and Aristotle says that the physician should be a bit sickly himself, to better understand the symptoms of his patients.[35]

This would prompt us to think of the whale as Ahab's friend in a private relation, to use Carl Schmitt's terms of reference. He is not the public enemy. Ahab at once loves and hates him, as one might love and hate a friend. Ahab's charisma is such that he bends the crew to his will, and makes them act as if the whale were Public Enemy Number One, and they represent the people in an act of war. The main merit of these emphases is that they remind us that we are reading a work of fiction, not a tract or an editorial. If the whale represents "no continuous relation between art and nature," as Frye holds, then we are more than ever justified in removing the allegory and thinking of the book in aesthetic terms. This would entail distancing ourselves from the zeitgeist the White House has prescribed. But that is not impossible. We may still engage in ruses, as Michel de Certeau recommended in *The Practice of Everyday Life:* "the ruses of other interests and desires that are neither determined nor captured by the systems in which they develop."[36]

The question of the art of *Moby-Dick* is still open. We would do well to start again with Blackmur on that issue. We are under no obligation to construe the book in the darkness of a Cold War or Hot War program. Let journalists and historians argue about that. A further merit of Frye and Burke on *Moby-Dick* is that they shift the interpretive center of the book from Ahab and Ishmael to Ahab and the white whale. This has the effect of displacing Ishmael to the margin, where he belongs. If the first sentence of the book were not "Call me Ishmael," we would not think of giving him the compositional privilege he has attained. He is not an adequate character to sustain the cultural role the Cold War rhetoric forced upon him, or indeed any other cultural or political paradigm. But then the Cold War critics should not have turned the book into a parable at all.

So far as I know, answers to Blackmur have taken two forms. Herbert G. Eldridge has argued that *Moby-Dick* did not emerge haphazardly from a process of vagary; it is strictly composed on a principle of numerical correspondence. The book mimes the voyage it describes, and proceeds in accordance with the six oceans it traverses:

> Various routes would be possible, but Melville takes the *Pequod* irregularly across and down the Atlantic to Good Hope, across the Indian Ocean to Sumatra and through the Sunda Strait, through the Java and China seas, into the Pacific to the Japanese whaling grounds, and east-

> southeast to the equatorial grounds for the fatal confrontation with Moby Dick.

The six sections are these: (1) New Bedford and Nantucket, chapters 1 to 22. (2) Nantucket to the Cape of Good Hope, chapters 23 to 50. (3) Good Hope to Sunda Strait, chapters 51 to 86. (4) Sunda Strait to Pacific, chapters 87 to 110. (5) Pacific to Equator, chapters 111 to 129. (6) Equator, chapters 130 to 135. Eldridge also maintains that "at the numerical center of all six divisions are traces of craft clearly identifiable through peculiarities of style, technique, episode, and theme and suggesting a measured subdivision of the voyage outline."[37] Melville apparently worked with such an outline and arranged a certain symmetry of parts. He did not submit to whatever occurred to him or to the "organic" disposition of materials he described in chapter 63: "Out of the trunk, the branches grow: out of them, the twigs. So, in productive subjects, grow the chapters."[38] But Eldridge's reading doesn't meet Blackmur's argument. If Melville worked with an outline, it is strange that he let the detail of the book run in fits and starts and sometimes pitched it into contradiction. The devices that Eldridge describes don't refute Blackmur's claim that Melville "was only a story teller betimes, for illustrative or apologetic or evangelical purposes," and that he never mastered "dramatic form with its inspiriting conventions."[39] True, Blackmur's concept of fiction was Jamesian, "dramatic form" being a primary imperative according to James.

A second answer to Blackmur is found in William Spanos's book, though that is not its main concern. The main concern is ontological and political. Spanos, a scholar of Heidegger and Derrida, speaks of Ahab's representation of the whale in man's image as gathering Being at large "in all its temporal and spatial multiplicity" into a concentrated image of universal Evil. By this means, Melville discloses "the latent violence against difference informing the 'benign' logic of the Emersonian myth of 'Central' or 'Representative Man.'" The political consequence of this violence is seen in "the self-destruction of the logic of the sovereign subject," which explains the American interventions in Vietnam, Afghanistan, and Iraq. Spanos's book is an essay in Deconstruction, invoking Nietzsche, Heidegger, and Derrida to interrogate the metaphysical tradition from Plato to Husserl on which the Western project of knowledge-as-power has proceeded: "In Nietzsche's terms, Captain Ahab's single-minded pursuit of the white whale is ultimately motivated by the will to power over being that repeats Western logocentric Man's—the Old Adam's, as it were—resentful nihilistic obsession to revenge himself against the transience of time." Ahab is mad, Spanos says, but so is the West and for the same reason, because it rages to recover identity from difference, eternity from time, stillness from motion. Ishmael is sane because he accepts the whale as—in Spanos's terms—"a manifestation of being's unspeakable mystery." Ishmael understands, but does not share, Ahab's totalizing demand "to find a single, all-encompassing object for dread—a scapegoat—and thus to familiarize and contain the uncanny." He remains—it is Spanos's highest praise—"a nameless orphan, a centerless self in a Fatherless and decentered world."[40]

Spanos sounds like a Matthiessen-after-Derrida, but he does not offer Ishmael as the saving grace of American culture. His book is a formidable reply to Blackmur's neo-Jamesian dismissal of *Moby-Dick.* It has the merit of removing *Moby-Dick* from its entanglement in the rhetoric of the Cold or the Hot War and giving us another thoughtful reading of it. The only problem with its argument—but it is a considerable one—is that it assimilates the book to a program of Deconstruction just as predictable as Matthiessen's propaganda. It is hard to believe that *Moby-Dick* anticipates Beckett's *Watt* and that Melville knew that that was what he was doing: undermining the stability of characters, refuting "presence," and mocking the semblances of a story. Hard, too, to watch with incredulity as Spanos turns poor, limited, nearly-suppressed Ishmael into a Derrida. But it is something to have given us another form of fiction that *Moby-Dick* might be thought to fulfill, after many years in which we were allowed only to choose between its being a great, failed novel or a dangerously pliable romance.

Spanos argues, against Blackmur, that the errancy of *Moby-Dick* is not due to Melville's incompetence or waywardness; it is a deliberate assault on the metaphysical visions of tragedy and romance which take knowledge, presence, and meaning as their consoling axioms:

> Far from writing or failing to write a novel that enacts the encompassing epiphanic closure of tragedy, Melville wrote a novel that exists to destroy not simply the idea of tragedy but the *metaphysical vision* that has given privileged status to tragic form, indeed, to *all* structurally teleological literary forms—including what came to be called the American romance—grounded in the certainty of an ultimate presence and a determinate meaning.[41]

Moby-Dick is therefore parody or, in Bakhtin's term, carnival, a travesty of the Jamesian well-made novel with its compositional duty, its self-presence, sovereign characters, and point of view. Spanos would have us take this passage from *Pierre* as Melville's motto:

> While the countless tribes of common knowledge laboriously spin vails of mystery, only to complacently clear them up at last . . . yet the profounder emanations of the human mind, intended to illustrate all that can be humanly known of human life, these never unravel their own intricacies, and have no proper endings, but in imperfect, unanticipated, and disappointing sequels (as mutilated stumps), hurry to abrupt intermergings with the eternal tides of time and fate.[42]

Or in the version given by Ishmael: "There are some enterprises in which a careful disorderliness is the true method."[43] It follows that Spanos would take the harm out of Pease's presentation of

Ishmael as a totalitarian master of rhetoric. Ishmael's rhetorical escapades are not sinister, according to Spanos; they are Derridean flourishes to preserve "the freeplay of his mind against the imperial imperatives of logocentric structure."[44]

I suppose Spanos has in view such a chapter as "The Prairie," in which Ishmael—or call him Melville, for the moment—dallies his way into charm and gesture:

> Genius in the Sperm Whale? Has the Sperm Whale ever written a book, spoken a speech? No, his great genius is declared in his doing nothing particular to prove it. It is moreover declared in his pyramidical silence. And this reminds me that had the great Sperm Whale been known to the young Orient World, he would have been deified by their child-magian thoughts. They deified the crocodile of the Nile, because the crocodile is tongueless; and the Sperm Whale has no tongue, or at least it is so exceedingly small, as to be incapable of protrusion. If hereafter any highly cultured, poetical nation shall lure back to their birth-right, the merry May-day gods of old; and livingly enthrone them again in the now egotistical sky; in the now unhaunted hill; then be sure, exalted to Jove's high seat, the great Sperm Whale shall lord it.
>
> Champollion deciphered the wrinkled granite hieroglyphics. But there is no Champollion to decipher the

> Egypt of every man's and every being's face. Physiognomy, like every other human science, is but a passing fable. If then, Sir William Jones, who read in thirty languages, could not read the simplest peasant's face in its profounder and more subtle meanings, how may unlettered Ishmael hope to read the awful Chaldee of the Sperm Whale's brow? I but put that brow before us. Read it if you can.[45]

It is gorgeous nonsense. To find anything like it, we have to go to the seventeenth century stylists, to Browne and Burton, with their mercurial whimsies and gravities. If we call it Derridean freeplay, we can think of the formal progressions it fends off. None of these is damaged. Science remains untouched, it is whatever it was before Ishmael starting passing the time, rambling on. We enjoy his rigmarole, short of turning the book into an anthology of conceits. No one will challenge him to explicate the "now egotistical sky" or "the now unhaunted hill." The contrast between this genial doodling and Ahab's lunacy of one idea is an attribute, not the least, of *Moby-Dick*. But it is a diversion from the main issues, from good and evil interpenetrated, according to Matthew 13, Christ's parable of the good seed and the tares that are allowed to grow together till harvesttime, "the end of the world," when—but not before—they will be justly separated in their kinds; a diversion, too, from the opacity of life itself and the necessity of our being more or less blank in the face of it.

So much for another reading of *Moby-Dick,* however partial. But no book stays whole in one's mind. We remember fragments of it, not necessarily the fundamental bits. Of *Hamlet* I recall most vividly not the great episodes but a couple of lines of Ophelia's short soliloquy in the first scene of the third act which fill up the time after Hamlet's exit and before the King and Polonius come in: "O, woe is me,/T' have seen what I have seen, see what I see!" Now that *Moby-Dick* has receded into my irregular sense of it, I find that what comes forward with the name is a passage in chapter 96, "The Try-Works," where Ishmael has been describing the pagan harpooners, among the flames, stoking the try-works with blubber. He denounces carefree men and insists that the truest man is the Man of Sorrows. I'll transcribe the passage:

> But even Solomon, he says, "the man that wandereth out of the way of understanding shall remain" (*i.e.* even while living) "in the congregation of the dead." Give not thyself up, then, to fire, lest it invert thee, deaden thee; as for the time it did me. There is a wisdom that it woe; but there is a woe that is madness. And there is a Catskill eagle in some souls that can alike dive down into the blackest gorges, and soar out of them again and become invisible in the sunny spaces. And even if he for ever flies within the gorge, that gorge is in the mountains; so that even in his lowest swoop the mountain eagle is still higher than other birds upon the plain, even though they soar.[46]

The *i.e.* interruption is awkward. Ishmael does not speak in a printer's parenthesis. Let that pass. Air in *Moby-Dick* is the feminine element, the sea being masculine, correlations given in chapter 132, "The Symphony." If the Catskill eagle is sustained by the air while still exercising its freedom, the image is as complete as Melville can make it. Ahab is not referred to, there is no need to be explicit. The passage makes no concession to the human world in terms of content. Of the four elements, it moves beyond three —earth, fire, and water—and it exhibits in the providential fourth that exact congruence of feeling and form which is Melville's theme, if mainly by default.

3

The Scarlet Letter

> Leave him alone for a moment or two,
> and you'll see him with his head
> bent down, brooding, brooding,
> eyes fixed on some chip,
> some stone, some common plant,
> the commonest thing,
> as if it were the clue.
> The disturbed eyes rise,
> furtive, foiled, dissatisfied
> from meditation on the true
> and insignificant.
>
> —Robert Lowell, "Hawthorne"

I

When I first read *The Scarlet Letter*, I found it bewildering. That impression has not entirely receded, but I think I understand how it came about and why it has to some extent persisted. The title of the book implied a story about sin—a scarlet woman—and indeed the book often refers to sin and sinfulness; but none of the characters has a convinced sense of sin. Hawthorne seems to equivocate among the values he brings forward. I acknowledge, without regarding the acknowledgment as a major concession, that my understanding of sin is the one I was taught in Catholic elementary and secondary schools in Northern Ireland. In the Christian Brothers School in Newry, where I was a day pupil, I was instructed that a sin is "any thought, word, or deed contrary to the Law of God." A mortal sin is "a thought, word, or deed which violates one of the essential prescriptions of God's law, and results in the loss of His friendship and of sanctifying grace." I was supposed to know God's law by maintaining an alert conscience and by accepting the teaching of the Catholic Church. Committing a grave sin, I break my relation to God, which remains ideal, an axiom of faith, till it is activated by prayer and the sacraments, especially penance and the eucharist. I estrange myself from God in the most drastic way by committing a mortal sin. Three conditions are required that a sin be mortal: "grave matter, full advertence to what one is doing (perfect knowledge), and full consent of the will."[1]

When I left secondary school, I went to Dublin as an undergraduate student at University College. There I exacerbated my sense of sin by reading with notable intensity the novels of Joyce, Graham Greene, François Mauriac, and Georges Bernanos. I had not yet read Andre Dubus's "Adultery," a story that might have had much the same effect on me. I recall with particular clarity *The Diary of a Country Priest* and the conviction of sin it exposed. Joyce was even closer to home. In the fourth chapter of *A Portrait of the Artist as a Young Man* Stephen Dedalus is pondering the priest's suggestion that he might have a vocation to the priesthood, but he reflects at the same time that the priest's appeal has not really touched him:

> He was destined to learn his own wisdom apart from others or to learn the wisdom of others himself wandering among the snares of the world.
>
> The snares of the world were its ways of sin. He would fall. He had not yet fallen but he would fall silently, in an instant. Not to fall was too hard, too hard: and he felt the silent lapse of his soul, as it would be at some instant to come, falling, falling but not yet fallen, still unfallen but about to fall.[2]

Those sentences had for me the true scholastic clarity. They enforced a sense of sin which survives every urge on Stephen's part to make it yield to the aesthetic swoon of syllables, "falling but not yet fallen." The snares of the world were not merely figurative, as if fulfilling the logic of "wandering"; they waited to trap you into sin. When I read Greene's *The Heart of the Matter,* I found Scobie's sense of sin so acute, unbeliever as in many respects he is, that I could even understand the moment in which he feels as temptation the possibility of doing the right thing: giving up his mistress, going to confession, and taking communion. His mistress Helen Rolt is so blank that she can't appreciate what it means for Scobie to be doomed to believe that he is in a state of sin:

> "Well then," she said triumphantly, "be hung for a sheep. You are in—what do you call it?—mortal sin?—now. What difference does it make?"
>
> He thought: pious people, I suppose, would call this the devil speaking, but he knew that evil never spoke in these crude answerable terms: that was innocence. He said, "there *is* a difference—a big difference. It's not easy to explain. *Now* I'm just putting our love above—well, my safety. But the other—the other's really evil. It's like the Black Mass, the man who steals the sacrament to desecrate it. It's striking God when he's down—in my power."

Scobie can't bring himself to name the other sin he's referring to. It's blasphemy, as my Catholic education made clear, a sin against the Holy Ghost, far worse than the adultery he has committed so often with Helen. When he goes to Mass with his wife and takes communion, he knows what he has done. He says to Helen:

> I believe that I'm damned for all eternity—unless a miracle happens. . . . What I've done is far worse than murder—that's an act, a blow, a stab, a shot: it's over and done, but I'm carrying my corruption around with me. It's the coating of my stomach.[3]

I had no problem understanding Scobie. I found it more difficult to understand Helen's assured secular blankness, her inability to imagine what it would be to sin.

When I read *The Scarlet Letter,* I could not avoid feeling that Hawthorne, speaking of sin and sinfulness, had in view nothing as specific as Scobie's adultery and blasphemy. When he referred to sin, he seemed to assume a force of evil so pervasive that it did not need to be embodied in anyone or in any action in particular. It was all general and vague, though it might be found consequential in families and generations, as in *The House of the Seven Gables.* The primary assumption was that God did not come into it: my soul's relation to God was not an issue. According to Hawthorne, even on the Day of Judgment, "man's own inexorable Judge will be himself, and the punishment of his sins will be the perception of them."[4] Neither Hester Prynne nor Arthur Dimmesdale acknowledges that adultery is a sin and that they stand in danger of eternal damnation: they have not repented, confessed their sin, or prayed for forgiveness. As late as chapter 18, after the scene in the forest, Dimmesdale resolves to accept Hester's plan, abandon the community, and make a new life with Hester and Pearl in Europe. There is not a hint of remorse, contrition, or confession. Hester throws away the scarlet letter and lets her hair fall over her shoulders. "See! With this symbol, I undo it all, and make it as it had never been!" The chapter is called "A Flood of Sunshine," and the sun comes out to rejoice that the decision has been made, the lovers are together again now and for the apparent future:

> Such was the sympathy of Nature—that wild, heathen Nature of the forest, never subjugated by human law, nor illumined by higher truth—with the bliss of these two spirits! Love, whether newly born, or aroused from a deathlike slumber, must always create a sunshine, filling the heart so full of radiance, that it overflows upon the outward world.

It overflows, too, apparently, upon the sin these lovers have committed and intend to commit again. The narrator—we may call this figure Hawthorne—seems to insist that love and nature are insuperable values and that morality has nothing to say to them. When Dimmesdale agrees to Hester's plan, Hawthorne writes:

> The decision once made, a glow of strange enjoyment threw its flickering brightness over the trouble of his breast. It was the exhilarating effect—upon a prisoner just escaped from the dungeon of his own heart—of breathing the wild, free atmosphere of an unredeemed, unchristianized, lawless region. His spirit rose, as it were, with a bound, and attained a nearer prospect of the sky, than throughout all the misery which had kept him grovelling on the earth. Of a deeply religious temperament, there was inevitably a tinge of the devotional in his mood.
>
> "Do I feel joy again?" cried he, wondering at himself. "Methought the germ of it was dead in me! O Hester,

> thou art my better angel! I seem to have flung myself—sick, sin-stained, and sorrow-blackened—down upon these forest-leaves, and to have risen up all made anew, and with new powers to glorify Him that hath been merciful? This is already the better life! Why did we not find it sooner?[5]

All they have done is spend some hours in the forest rather than in the town, and enact a little pastoral of life without law. But that is enough. They have invoked the authority of the natural world and repudiated the Puritan law of their community, the settlement, the town.

True, Hawthorne was not an Irish Catholic. But in *The Scarlet Letter* he invented two characters—Hester and Arthur—who did not believe that what they had done was a sin. On the contrary. "What we did had a consecration of its own," Hester says to Dimmesdale. "We felt it so! We said so to each other. Hast thou forgotten it?" and even though Dimmesdale subdues her intensity—"Hush, Hester!"—he also says, "No; I have not forgotten!" That leaves open the question of Hawthorne's ability to imagine what it would be—or what it meant in the New England of the mid-seventeenth century—to commit a mortal sin. If Nature and the sun are deemed to bless adultery, what is the status of law? The sexual character of the relation between Hester and Dimmesdale is so vaguely rendered that only the existence of Pearl as a consequence of it makes it credible. But even if we add our own erotic imagination to Hawthorne's equivocation, it is still the case that Hawthorne conceives of sin as a social transgression only, an act by which I isolate myself from the community to which I belong. That was not a consideration in Newry. I was taught to respect "the communion of saints," the spiritual solidarity that binds together the faithful on earth, the souls in purgatory, and the saints in heaven in the organic unity of the mystical body under Christ its head, but by committing a sin I was not conscious of offending the communion of saints, I was offending God alone. My relation to God was mediated by the sacraments of the Church, not by any community to which I belonged. In Hawthorne, the terms of reference and rebuke are entirely social. The transgression is committed against the Puritan community. It is an act of pride and it becomes even more scandalous if, like Dimmesdale, I keep it secret. The community takes the place of God, according to the practice of a people "amongst whom religion and law," as Hawthorne says, "were almost identical." The forms of authority in New England during the years of the story —1642 to 1649—"were felt to possess the sacredness of divine institutions," but the understanding of "sacredness" and "divine" in that sentence—or in the community to which it refers—was already, it appears, diminished, it was dwindling into a habit of social and civic life.[6] If religion and law were almost one and the same, that one was almost entirely law. The sense of evil was moving from theology and morality to sociology. Evil was incorrigible because no social institution could accommodate it. The Puritan community as Hawthorne depicts it was strikingly impoverished in ritual and symbolism, in its sense of the sacred, the transcendent, the numinous. The world according to Puritanism was ceasing to be sacred.

Hawthorne had no trouble imagining universal evil—Original Sin without the theology of it. In "Earth's Holocaust" he attributes evil to a defect of "the Heart." "The Heart—the Heart—there was the little, yet boundless sphere, wherein existed the original wrong, of which the crime and misery of this outward world were merely types." Purify that inner sphere, the narrator of "Earth's Holocaust" says, "and the many shapes of evil that haunt the outward, and which now seem almost our only realities, will turn to shadowy phantoms, and vanish of their own accord."[7] In chapter 42 of *The Marble Faun* Hilda and Kenyon talk about the possibly fortunate aspects of the Fall—the paradoxical *felix culpa*—and Miriam comes back to the question in conversation with Donatello and Kenyon in chapter 47, but in the end Hawthorne lets the possibility drift out of sight. But if a defect of "the Heart" accounts for "the original wrong," Hawthorne seems to have no capacity to imagine actual sin, the guilt of it, and the hope of forgiveness. He could imagine the Devil, but not his works, their manifestation in particular acts. If you compare Hawthorne's sense of sin with the Puritan Thomas Hooker's, as in the sermon on "A True Sight of Sin," you find that Hooker's sight of it is far more acute:

> Now by sin we jostle the law out of its place and the Lord out of His glorious sovereignty, pluck the crown from his head and the scepter out of His hand; and we say and profess by our practice, there is not authority and power there to govern, nor wisdom to guide, nor good to content me, but I will be swayed by mine own will and led by mine own deluded reason and satisfied with my own lusts.[8]

Those are words of almost Catholic particularity: "jostle," "pluck," "swayed," "led," "satisfied." The worst that Hawthorne can say of sin in *The Scarlet Letter* is that it is psychologically damaging to the sinner and that the damage can't be repaired. Hester knows why she has been ostracized: she has incurred social disgrace and the punishment of being for a time cast aside. But she does not feel guilty. Nor does Dimmesdale: his actions are occluded by his hypocrisy. Even in his last hours, he convicts himself not of actual sin but of sharing the universal sinfulness of mankind. In the conclusion the narrator reports that according to certain "highly respectable witnesses," Dimmesdale "had desired, by yielding up his breath in the arms of that fallen woman, to express to the world how utterly nugatory is the choicest of man's own righteousness." It is a moral lesson so general that no particular soul need tremble on learning it. After exhausting life "in his efforts for mankind's spiritual good, Dimmesdale had made the manner of his death a parable, in order to impress on his admirers the mighty and mournful lesson, that, in the view of Infinite Purity, we are sinners all alike."[9] That is for Infinite Purity to say, not for Dimmesdale. In "The Minister's Black Veil" Hawthorne keeps talking about Parson Hooper's secret sin without saying what it is. I agree with William Empson that it can only be an addiction to masturbation and that readers are expected to know "quite well what it all means." The appearance of being ambiguous is therefore "an insinuating pretence."[10] Not only does Hawthorne keep talking about the sin, but Hooper does: his most memorable sermon is on secret sin, "and those sad mysteries which we hide from our nearest and dearest, and would fain conceal from our own consciousness, even forgetting that the Omniscient can detect them." But the fact that the Omniscient can detect my sins is no strong reason for me to broadcast them to the neighborhood. "If I hide my face for sorrow," Hooper says, "there is cause enough, . . . and if I cover it for secret sin, what mortal might not do the same?" This may be true, or it may not:

> "Why do you tremble at me alone?" cried he, turning his veiled face round the circle of pale spectators. "Tremble also at each other! Have men avoided me, and women shown no pity, and children screamed and fled, only for my black veil? What, by the mystery which it obscurely typifies, has made this piece of crape so awful? When the friend shows his inmost heart to his friend; the lover to his best-beloved; when man does not vainly

> shrink from the eye of his Creator, loathsomely treasuring up the secret of his sin; then deem me a monster, for the symbol beneath which I have lived, and die! I look around me, and, lo! on every visage a Black Veil!"[11]

This may just mean: "everybody masturbates." But at that moment, Hooper should not be looking around him or comparing his black veil with other black veils that should be there. Besides, the parable is specious, if we take it in the ominously universal sense that Hooper seems to intend. Despite the view attributed to Infinite Purity, we are not sinners all alike, Charles Manson is not the same as Mother Teresa, Chillingworth is not the same as Hester and Dimmesdale. Dimmesdale knows this, at least on one occasion: "We are not, Hester, the worst sinners in the world. There is one worse than even the polluted priest! That old man's revenge has been blacker than my sin. He has violated, in cold blood, the sanctity of a human heart. Thou and I, Hester, never did so!"[12] The theology of Original Sin does not hold that in our actual sins we are sinners indistinguishable from one another.

To Hawthorne, it appears that a sin is an act, a condition, a state of consciousness such that I will not reveal it to my community—or indeed to anyone. The sin consists in my refusal to come clean and to tell the neighbors what I have done. It is Ethan Brand's unpardonable sin. It is also Hooper's, because he refuses to disclose it to his community, least of all to his fiancée Elizabeth. He keeps postponing marriage forever on the grounds that "there is an hour to come when all of us shall cast aside our veils. Take it not amiss, beloved friend, if I wear this piece of crape till then." Beloved friend takes it amiss, as Hooper evidently knew she would: so there will be no marriage. But Hooper doesn't resign his ministry. His election sermon is so impressive that "the legislative measures of that year, were characterized by all the gloom and piety of our earliest ancestral sway."[13] Empson takes these "carefully chosen words" to mean that Hooper induced his community leaders "to burn witches again" and to let the people "gloat over tortures."[14] I don't see how the words could be interpreted otherwise. Hawthorne equivocates again in *The Marble Faun*. Hilda goes to confession, though she is not a Catholic, but the confession is a travesty: what she has to tell the priest is no sin of her own but Miriam's. When the priest asks her, with just asperity, what she thinks she is doing in the confessional, Hilda grasps at the nearest excuse: "It seemed as if I made the awful guilt my own, by keeping it hidden in my heart."[15] Dimmesdale reveals his sin at the last moment, and is saved by his dying from the punishment that should follow the confession. He is redeemed, in a sense, but he does not suffer punishment in the communal terms in which he committed the sin; except for the consideration, grave indeed, that the community will not remember him as a saint. In a modern retelling of the story of *The Scarlet Letter*—the film *The Crime of Padre Amaro*—the priest keeps his secret from the community and gets away with it, even to the extent of continuing to be revered as a holy man. Hawthorne's Hester is punished by the community she has offended: she has not been able to keep her secret, Pearl being the evidence of her sin. According to Hawthorne, the concealment is more lethal than the sin concealed; because it undermines the community and makes it impossible, even for the individual, to know which of his faces is the true one—if any of them can be true, given the concealment. As Hawthorne writes in *The Scarlet Letter:* "No man, for any considerable period, can wear one face to himself, and another to the multitude, without finally getting bewildered as to which may be the true."[16] Secrecy defines sin in the only form that matters. Hawthorne is apparently unable or unwilling to imagine a sin in any other terms.

Two possible interpretations suggest themselves. One is that he was fully capable of imagining actual sin but, in presenting Hester and Dimmesdale, chose not to. According to this view, the main nuance of the book consists in the fact that the sinful characters—or rather one of them, Hester, since Dimmesdale's public confession is made too late to affect the course of things—are condemned by the community to which they belong, but are not guilty in their own eyes. As in the forest, they appeal beyond culture to Nature, which has no thought of sin. The second possibility is that Hawthorne was indeed incapable of imagining an actual sin as distinct from universal—and universally vague—evil, Adam's curse falling indiscriminately on the entire human race. This seems to me more telling. It is worth noting how often in Hawthorne's fiction a character who might be thought to have committed a sin appeals beyond the deed to the incorrigible action of Fate. In *The Marble Faun* the evil specter that haunts Miriam tells her, in chapter 11, that they are bound together by fate: "But, Miriam, believe me, it is not your fate to die, while there remains so much to be sinned and suffered in the world. We have a destiny, which we must needs fulfil together."[17] In chapter 14 of *The Scarlet Letter* Hester begs Chillingworth to forgive her and Dimmesdale:

> "Peace, Hester, peace!" replied the old man, with gloomy sternness. "It is not granted me to pardon. I have no such power as thou tellest me of. My old faith, long forgotten, comes back to me, and explains all that we do, and all we suffer. By that first step awry, thou didst plant the germ of evil; but, since that moment, it has all been a dark necessity. Ye that have wronged me are not sinful, save in a kind of typical illusion; neither am I fiend-like, who have snatched a fiend's office from his hands. It is our fate. Let the black flower blossom as it may![18]

Chillingworth recites this version of Calvinism in his own favor, even though he offers it equally to Hester and Dimmesdale, who have not asked for it.

2

In the years since I first read *The Scarlet Letter* I have noted a few accounts of Hawthorne which propose to explain why his sense of universal evil was far more pronounced than his sense of actual sin. Two of these call for particular consideration. In his monograph on Hawthorne, Henry James claims that "the Puritan strain in his blood ran clear," and that to Hawthorne as to his ancestors "the consciousness of *sin* was the most importunate fact of life." James comes back to that emphasis forty pages later when he speaks of the purity, spontaneity, and naturalness of Hawthorne's fancy. It is interesting, James says, to see how "the imagination, in this capital son of the old Puritans, reflected the hue of the purely moral part, of the dusky, overshadowed conscience." That conscience," by no fault of its own, in every genuine offshoot of that sombre lineage, lay under the shadow of the sense of *sin*." But as he takes up the theme, James removes the shadow of the sense of sin by arguing that it formed merely one of the conditions of Hawthorne's art and that, within limits, Hawthorne was free to act upon it as he wished. It turns out that among the possible ways of acting upon it, Hawthorne's was the best, "for he contrived, by an exquisite process, best known to himself, to transmute this heavy moral burden into the very substance of the imagination, to make it evaporate in the light and charming fumes of artistic production." Nothing is more curious and interesting, James claims, "than this almost exclusively *imported* character of the sense of sin in Hawthorne's mind; it seems to exist there merely for an artistic or literary purpose." Hawthorne's relation to his inheritance, the Puritan conscience, was "only, as one may say, intellectual; it was not moral and theological." He played with it:

> He was not discomposed, disturbed, haunted by it, in the manner of its usual and regular victims, who had not the little postern door of fancy to slip through, to the other side of the wall. It was, indeed, to his imaginative vision, the great fact of man's nature; the light element that had been mingled with his own composition always clung to this rugged prominence of moral responsibility, like the mist that hovers about the mountain.

In this strange monograph, James is determined to present Hawthorne's genius as light and airy, and to say that it is beautiful to the degree of its playfulness. He speaks of Hawthorne's imagination taking license to amuse itself, even to the extent of converting the principle of the Puritan conscience into one of his toys. "When he was lightest at heart, he was most creative," James claims. Hawthorne judged "the old Puritan moral sense, the consciousness of sin and hell, of the fearful nature of our responsibilities and the savage character of our Taskmaster," from the poetic and aesthetic point of view—which James describes in this case dismissively as "the point of view of entertainment and irony." The absence of conviction, James says, "makes the difference; but the difference is great." It shows itself in "Young Goodman Brown," a magnificent romance that "evidently means nothing as regards Hawthorne's own state of mind, his conviction of human depravity and his consequent melancholy; for the simple reason that if it meant anything, it would mean too much." James does not say that Hawthorne's imagination was cynical, but he allows us to infer that it was, and that the airy quality of his mind was consistent with his decision to acknowledge his inherited burdens mainly by taking them lightly and putting them aside. His Puritan precursors, in James's spirited account of them, were "a handful of half-starved fanatics." That they played a part in "laying the foundations of a mighty empire" is true enough and much in their favor, but the truth once acknowledged is sufficiently attested: it is not necessary to keep on thanking them. Hawthorne, according to James, saw no reason to be forever afflicted by the New England to which he felt himself natively bound. James is even prepared to include Hawthorne's recourse to romance, allegory, and symbolism in the list of devices for lightness. It was as if Hawthorne released himself from the burdens of realism—of living up to the responsibilities of that genre—by turning to romance, allegory, and symbolism, which James regards as among the lighter resolves of literature. Readers who like those forms of fiction, James maintains, enjoy having a story told "as if it were another and a very different story."[19] Hawthorne is made to appear almost debonair.

It is not surprising that James condescended to Hawthorne and thought of him as a first draft of what a major American novelist might be. It is hard to avoid the conclusion, reading James's monograph, that it was Hawthorne's highest honor that he was superseded, in every respect that mattered, by Henry James. This is the implication, apparently, of Hawthorne's recourse to the poetic and the aesthetic devices: they delivered him from heavy matters into charming instances of weightlessness. This interpretation has proved persuasive to some readers, including Q. D. Leavis, who thinks it splendid, apparently, that Hawthorne escaped from religion into the deeper psychology. Writing of "Young Goodman Brown," she says:

> Hawthorne has imaginatively recreated for the reader that Calvinist sense of sin, that theory which did in actuality shape the early social and spiritual history of New England. But in Hawthorne, by a wonderful feat of transmutation, it has no religious significance, it is as a psychological state that it is explored. Young Goodman Brown's Faith is not faith in Christ but faith in human beings, and losing it he is doomed to isolation forever.[20]

To move with such ease from a reference to the Calvinist sense of sin to a representation of it as a theory is to appreciate that Mrs. Leavis took a light-hearted view of it in any designation: the move from religion into psychology is to be seen as self-evidently a triumph.

But James's reading of Hawthorne has not been found decisive. We are inclined to read Hawthorne's fictions differently and to have "Young Goodman Brown" mean too much rather than that it should mean nothing. But the charge of an absence of conviction on Hawthorne's part is hard to refute, if it is a charge rather than, as James seems to hold, an engaging trait. If we think of it in cultural and historical terms, it makes a difference of two hundred years during which the American sense of sin nearly disappeared in the Unitarianism that was as much of Christianity as Hawthorne was prepared to maintain. Hawthorne makes this clear in a passage from "Main Street." He has been referring to the earliest settlement in New England and praising his good fortune that he did not have to live there:

> Happy are we, if for nothing else, yet because we did not live in those days. In truth, when the first novelty and stir of spirit had subsided,—when the new settlement, between the forest-border and the sea, had become actually a little town,—its daily life must have trudged onward with hardly anything to diversify and enliven it, while also its rigidity could not fail to cause miserable distortions of the moral nature. Such a life was sinister to the intellect, and sinister to the heart; especially when one generation had bequeathed its religious gloom, and the counterfeit of its religious ardor, to the next; for these characteristics, as was inevitable, assumed the form both of hypocrisy and exaggeration, by being inherited from the example and precept of other human beings, and not from an original and spiritual source.

Hawthorne's reference to "the counterfeit of its religious ardor" shows more malice than one would have anticipated. He seems to think, in those last sentences, that everyone should invent a new religion every morning—which is probably what Hawthorne deduced from Emerson's conversations. He rounds out the reflection:

> The sons and grandchildren of the first settlers were a race of lower and narrower souls than their progenitors had been. The latter were stern, severe, intolerant, but not superstitious, not even fanatical; and endowed, if any men of that age were, with a far-seeing worldly sagacity. But it was impossible for the succeeding race to grow up, in Heaven's freedom, beneath the discipline which their gloomy energy of character had established; nor, it may be, have we even yet thrown off all the unfavorable influences which, among many good ones, were bequeathed to us by our Puritan forefathers. Let us thank God for having given us such ancestors; and let each successive generation thank him, not less fervently, for being one step further from them in the march of ages.[21]

The God who is to be thanked, apparently, might just as well be called the march of ages or the zeitgeist.

A second explanation for Hawthorne's equivocal sense of sin is implicit in Allen Tate's essay on Emily Dickinson, especially in the form in which it was expanded and in some details modified by R. P. Blackmur's essay on that poet. Taking the two essays together, their argument amounts to a brisk reading of American literary history in the persons of Hawthorne, Emerson, Dickinson, and Henry James. The gist of the case is that Emily Dickinson came at a time which may have been painful to her soul but was enabling to her poems; a time when the theocracy of New England had nearly collapsed but was still felt as sufficiently in force to be interrogated and challenged, mocked as often as respected. While it lasted and whether we approve of its having lasted or not, the theocracy had "an immense, incalculable value for literature: it dramatized the human soul." It gave meaning to life, "the life of pious and impious, of learned and vulgar alike." Tate notes that Puritanism could not be to Dickinson "what it had been to the generation of Cotton Mather—a body of absolute truths; it was an unconscious discipline timed to the pulse of her life."[22] Blackmur veers from Tate at this point: he does not believe that Puritanisam was for Dickinson an unconscious discipline or that the timing was right for her pulse:

> Spiritual meaning and psychic stability were no longer the unconscious look and deep gesture worn and rehearsed life-long; they required the agony of doubt and the trial of deliberate expression in specifically, willfully objective form. Faith was sophisticated, freed, and terrified—but still lived; imagination had suddenly to do all the work of embodying faith formerly done by habit, and to embody it with the old machinery so far as it could be used.

In such conditions, faith—in the hands of the individual and while the institutions of faith are crumbling—"becomes an imaginative experiment of which all the elements are open to new and even blasphemous combinations, and which is subject to the addition of new insights." It was as if Dickinson lived in the doldrums but could remember a time when the winds of doctrine blew with enough force to compel behavior; and in some degree still felt the winds blowing, though not compellingly. Puritanism was no longer much good as doctrine, insight, or received wisdom, but it was good enough to be teased, provoked, interrogated. The theocracy was still there as machinery, though feeble for any more personal purpose. As a result, Dickinson could have only an experimental relation to it; but that was what she needed, her sensibility being as it was. She came at the most fortunate moment for the poetry she had to write, "the poetry of sophisticated, eccentric vision," as Blackmur calls it. It had to be eccentric because it did not issue from a living and central tradition of faith and practice. But it had nearly commensurate advantages. Summing up a good deal of detail, Blackmur claims that "the great advantage for a poet to come at a time of disintegrating culture is [that] the actuality of what we are and what we believe is suddenly seen to be nearly meaningless as habit, and must, to be adequately known, be translated to the terms and modes of the imagination."[23] Not every poet can make the most of these conditions. Some poets wither when they find that the imagination has to do all the work for itself.

Emerson, according to this emphasis in Tate and Blackmur, hardly knew what he was doing, but he ended up removing any tragic possibilities from the culture he addressed. The effect of Emerson's doctrine of individualism is that "there is no drama in human character because there is no tragic fault."[24] There is no sin, no action for which anyone would think of seeking forgiveness. One of the most shocking passages in "Experience," I find, is this flourish of exoneration:

> We believe in ourselves as we do not believe in others. We permit all things to ourselves, and that which we call sin in others is experiment for us. . . . Saints are sad, because they behold sin (even when they speculate) from the point of view of the conscience, and not of the intellect; a confusion of thought. Sin, from the thought, is a diminution, or *less;* seen from the conscience or will, it is pravity or *bad.* The intellect names it shade, absence of light, and no essence. The conscience must feel it as essence, essential evil. That it is not; it has an objective existence, but no subjective.[25]

"Hawthorne alone in his time," Tate says, "kept pure, in the primitive terms, the primitive vision; he brings the puritan tragedy to its climax." Man, "measured by a great idea outside himself, is found wanting."[26] But the only evidence of this purity of vision is that Hawthorne kept looking back at a cultural milieu in nearly every respect intractable. Tate and Blackmur did not take Hawthorne as lightly as James did, or think of the aesthetic project as removing his burdens. It must count for something that he kept looking back, across a gap of two hundred years, and that his historical sense was more or less adequate to the looking. Blackmur thought that Hawthorne's devices enabled him to see a lot and to circumvent what he did not want to engage with directly: "Some say Hawthorne was a great student of evil; I think rather he studied how to avoid and ignore it by interposing the frames of his tales between evil and the experience of it."[27] Perhaps that is to say that Hawthorne saw evil as omnivorous but diffuse, and that his imagination was not willing to identify evil with its local manifestations. There had to be more evil at large than he could specify. But if Hawthorne rejected the world, he did not reject it blithely. Tate says:

> Mastery of the world by rejecting the world was the doctrine, even if it was not always the practice, of Jonathan Edwards and Cotton Mather. It is the meaning of fate in Hawthorne: his people are fated to withdraw from the world and to be destroyed. And it is one of the great themes of Henry James.[28]

But the theme was much diminished by the time it reached James:

> Between Hawthorne and James lies an epoch. The temptation to sin, in Hawthorne, is, in James, transformed into the temptation not to do the "decent

> thing." A whole world-scheme, a complete cosmic background, has shrunk to the dimensions of the individual conscience.[29]

Tate does not say that the individual conscience finds it possible to reduce spiritual doubt to misgiving, morality to successive judgments of taste, and the question of salvation to the achievement of a personal style in the world. Nor does he say, as M. H. Abrams does in *Natural Supernaturalism,* that in late-nineteenth-century and some twentieth-century writers the religious paradigms are remembered, only their content and the conviction that sustained them having lapsed; as we see if we go from reading Wordsworth to reading Wallace Stevens. In Stevens's "Sunday Morning" the machinery is still there, though the poem derides it; it is Christianity, "the grave of Jesus, where he lay," but the dominant speaker of the poem walks away from the grave, remarking merely that "we live in an old chaos of the sun."[30] The situation is the one that Hegel anticipated in the preface to *Phenomenology of Spirit* when he claimed that one's sensory power is "so fast rooted in earthly things" that it requires force to raise it:

> The Spirit shows itself as so impoverished that, like a wanderer in the desert craving a mere mouthful of water, it seems to crave for its refreshment only the bare feeling of the divine in general. By the little which now satisfies Spirit, we can measure the extent of its loss.[31]

Perhaps Hawthorne, too, decided that the Puritan theocracy, whatever its values were, was such that it must fail and must survive only in the equivocal lore of its early history. Or that it must take a secular, worldly form—Franklinism, we might as well call it—if it is to be invoked for what it once was. In 1937 T. S. Eliot wrote:

> In the Puritan morality that I remember, it was tacitly assumed that if one was thrifty, enterprising, intelligent, practical and prudent in not violating social conventions, one ought to have a happy and "successful" life. Failure was due to some weakness or perversity peculiar to the individual; but the decent man need have no nightmares. It is now rather more common to assume that all individual misery is the fault of "society," and is remediable by alterations from without. Fundamentally, the two philosophies, however different they may appear in operation, are the same. It seems to me that all of us, so far as we attach ourselves to created objects and surrender our wills to temporal ends, are eaten by the same worm.[32]

Hawthorne would not have put the case in those terms. He might not even have viewed such developments with Eliot's mixture of dismay and contempt.

Not that Hawthorne had a good word to say of New England Puritanism. In "The May-Pole of Merry Mount," "Endicott and the Red Cross," "Dr. Bullivant," "Main Street," and other stories and sketches—as we have seen—he associates it with unremitting joylessness and gloom, the Puritan sermons being "cruel torturings and twistings of trite ideas, disgusting by the wearisome ingenuity which constitutes their only merit."[33] But Hawthorne's operative values are nonetheless predicated on the community that received those ideas. It is as if he dreamed that a culture which thought of religion and law as one and the same might someday replace law with far more genial practices, resulting in what Durkheim called effervescence, the free vitality of people when they come together as a community. In "The May-Pole of Merry Mount" such a community is imagined in the festive practice of dance and freedom, nature and culture at one, religion incorporating for the day its emblems of the heathen carnival, including "an English priest, canonically dressed, yet decked with flowers, in heathen fashion, and wearing a chaplet of the native vine leaves." "By the riot of his rolling eye," Hawthorne reports, "and the pagan decorations of his holy garb, he seemed the wildest monster there, and the very Comus of the crew." But when the Puritans discover these mummeries—that Shakespearean comedy of the green world—their governor John Endicott destroys the festival and punishes the revelers. Hawthorne writes, in terms similar to those of chapter 18 of *The Scarlet Letter:*

> The future complexion of New England was involved in this important quarrel. Should the grisly saints establish

> their jurisdiction over the gay sinners, then would their spirits darken all the clime, and make it a land of clouded visages, of hard toil, of sermon and psalm, forever. But should the banner-staff of Merry Mount be fortunate, sunshine would break upon the hills, and flowers would beautify the forest, and late posterity do homage to the May-Pole![34]

Still, it is an imported carnival, as the reference to Comus makes clear: it is not indigenous to its culture. What goes on in the midnight forest of "Young Goodman Brown" is a malign fiesta equal and opposite to the dances at Merry Mount, and even if we think, with Blackmur, that "the Devil is in the Forest, but the forest is within and the devil is ourselves," the values to which Hawthorne appeals are communal and the question is the same one: what makes a good society?[35] Can any society accommodate one's nightmares, Goodman Brown's most appalling fears and desires?

Two forces it cannot accommodate: secrecy and egotism. It hardly matters what Reverend Hooper has done, in comparison with the insistence of his secrecy. Secrecy makes the social definition of life a sham. As for egotism: Hawthorne gives it a story to itself, according to which Roderick Elliston is brought to say: "'Could I, for one instant, forget myself, the serpent might not abide within me. It is my diseased self-contemplation that has engendered and nourished him!'" But before he reaches this degree of wisdom, Hawthorne makes a psychological generalization:

> All persons, chronically diseased, are egotists, whether the disease be of the mind or body; whether it be sin, sorrow, or merely the more tolerable calamity of some endless pain, or mischief among the cords of mortal life. Such individuals are made acutely conscious of a self, by the torture in which it dwells.

The only release for Roderick is in his wife's voice: "'Then forget yourself, my husband . . . forget yourself in the idea of another!'"[36]

If in Hawthorne's fiction, as I have been arguing, God has been replaced by the idea of community, how does Hawthorne find it possible to give the idea of community such privilege? Communities easily if not always turn into crowds, crowds into monsters, Nuremberg rallies, marches on Rome. Frazer's *The Golden Bough* and Canetti's *Crowds and Power* should be enough to make anyone skeptical about the sentimentalizing of a community. Durkheim thought that religion was the origin of society and that societies developed their own vital energy, which might take various forms, genial or violent. His sociology of effervescence is based on that vision. But in 1936 his associate Marcel Mauss worried that Durkheim and his pupils—Mauss included—had not sufficiently taken into account the communal forces that made Fascism possible and perhaps inevitable.[37] You could not take the harm out of Fascism and Nazism by calling them effervescent. In "My Kinsman, Major Molineux" the contagion of the crowd makes Robin join in the laughter, his laugh the loudest, mocking his kinsman, an old Englishman driven through the town in tar and feathers, humiliated, a spectacle. This may be a prophecy of the American War of Independence, and Robin's laughter a sign of the effervescence of colonial America. But however we interpret the story, Robin learns that he has become a stranger to himself, bewildered among his surroundings. He may stay in town and make his fortune without the patronage of his kinsman Major Molineux, but he has lost his innocence: the crowd has taken it from him. Perhaps it is a blessing, or may in time come to appear such. But it is also a painful lesson about individuals and communities.

I said at the beginning that Hawthorne equivocates among his values. Blackmur settles for thinking the allegory, even of *The Scarlet Letter*, is reductive, making a contrast with Dante's:

> In Dante's allegory every adventure is met and what is met signifies further than had been known or intended, in prospect endlessly. Dante commands us what to bring by the authority of what is there. Hawthorne allows us to put in what we will at our own or a lesser level. Dante's allegory gives force to our own words—and thus to our thoughts as they find words—that they never previously had. Hawthorne's allegory lets our words seem good enough as they are, so that at best they only pass for thought. Dante's allegory is constructive, Hawthorne's allegory is reductive. Even the allegory of *The Scarlet Letter* is reductive of the values concerned; it is in the twilit

> limbo of virtue and knowledge—*virtute e conoscenza*—not in the light and dark of the continuing enterprise.[38]

I would add only a remark, that equivocation and reductiveness amount to much the same thing, the same predicament. Neither of them can be in prospect endless. It appears that Hawthorne could not make up his mind whether the sense of community was good enough to live by at full stretch or only to fall back on. It was all he had, once he had replaced God by community and dissolved religion in psychology. Nor could he decide whether a sin was a fierce and willful act of the individual soul or merely a symptom, a shadow, of universal evil. Either way, he could not work his values or drive his allegory with force, like Dante's, not merely personal. Blackmur lets him rest on what he could do:

> We cannot always be about mastering life; it is altogether sweet to put life off and give it the lie, and it is altogether proper to reduce life to a little less than our own size by the pretense either that we are bigger than life or that we are outcast. Hawthorne is an excellent help to these refuges, the more so if his language and conventions differ from ours. It is like saying, "I love you," in French; it is not so very different and, the first time, much more charming.[39]

But the collocation here of "sweet" and "charming" makes Blackmur's Hawthorne indistinguishable from Henry James's, and lets us think that Hester's sin and Dimmesdale's are only social misdemeanors. If that were true, *The Scarlet Letter* would not be worth comparing—as I think it should be compared—with *Wuthering Heights*. There are crucial differences. In *Wuthering Heights* there is the life represented by Thrushcross Grange, and there is the more pervasive life proceeding in place and time, the apple-picking, the harvest, Linton's crocuses, Mrs. Dean sweeping the hearth, the sound of Gimmerton's chapel bells, the ousels. The surge of energy between Catherine and Heathcliff is to be felt in relation to those ordinary, seasonal activities, the lives that go along with other lives. There is nothing—nothing convincingly realized—to compare with that in *The Scarlet Letter*. Even the great romantic gestures in *The Scarlet Letter*, such as Hester's claim of consecration, are mild by comparison with Catherine's claim, in chapter 9, in her conversation with Nelly:

> It would degrade me to marry Heathcliff, now; so he shall never know how I love him; and that, not because he's handsome, Nelly, but because he's more myself than I am. . . . My love for Linton is like the foliage in the woods. Time will change it, I'm well aware, as winter changes the trees—my love for Heathcliff resembles the eternal rocks beneath—a source of little visible delight, but necessary. Nelly, I *am* Heathcliff—he's always, always in my mind—not as a pleasure, any more than I am always a pleasure to myself—but, as my own being.[40]

The violence of the revenge play of Heathcliff, Catherine, and Linton is voided, in *The Scarlet Letter,* by having the relation between Hester and Chillingworth cold from the beginning, and Hester's relation to Dimmesdale a thing apart, separate from Chillingworth's enmity toward Dimmesdale. By comparison with Emily Brontë's audacity, her extremity and reach of desire, Hawthorne is almost genteel; he seems to ask us to write some of the book on his behalf by intuiting the limits to which he is not willing to go. Some readers would say that he gives us enough to allow us to infer the rest. But if we think of inferring the rest, it is because we read him against himself, we detect his equivocations and try to resolve them. If we don't, we let him invoke, without interruption, values and entities in which he doesn't believe—God, sin, Hell, justice, law. Why does he keep using these sacred words, despite their not being sacred to him? His faith is nominal, deformed by bad faith. His appeal to Nature is factitious, a gesture of rhetorical virtuosity. Does he believe in anything? Or is he trying to imagine faith by miming its syllables? Frank Kermode has argued that Hawthorne's subject is "the degree to which withered 'bygones' must be a part of the present and future." They are, he says, "of the old world, types of it, whether they are human, vegetable, social—for armorial bearings are types, too, yet their owners preserve them, like genetic traits, into a plebeian future."[41] But it is not clear whether the bygones are already withered by the time Hawthorne comes to them or are withered now by the ambiguity of Hawthorne's contact with them. No value survives the equivocation of Hawthorne's interest in it. Empson regarded Hawthorne, at least the author of "The Minister's Black Veil," as a decadent writer. "Hawthorne is an aesthetic writer, I don't deny, a premature decadent, in fact; but I think the result is shockingly nasty."[42] Nietzsche thought that decadence consists in the repudiation of wholeness: the word pulls loose from the sentence, the sentence from the paragraph, the paragraph from the whole. Anything but the whole.

I do not claim that my reading of *The Scarlet Letter* articulates a common sense of the book. Talk of sin, repentance, and confession is alien to the "spirit of the age." I gather, on informal evidence, that most readers take the book as a parable of civil disobedience and revere Hester for exemplifying it and for triumphing over a community they regard as undemocratic, "un-American." Hester is to them our best ur-feminist. She defies the community and survives, because the Puritan opposition to her is not something that Hawthorne takes seriously. The triumph is easy. Hester's sin is her glory, according to a facile politics in which theology is reduced to psychology, and morality to good fellowship. I see these reductions as meretricious.

There are many other ways of reading Hawthorne. One of these is to take him psychologically, setting aside the issues of sin, community, and God. Borges finds the stories—especially "Wakefield" and "Earth's Holocaust"—more compelling than the novels because he can enter into their psychological oddities without being restrained by historical and theological questions. In "Wakefield" a man's caprice is maintained for twenty years as if it were a resolve, and dropped just as arbitrarily. Borges had more to say about it than about *The Scarlet Letter*. Hawthorne's notebooks offer further enchantments. Many of the notes are so weird that we wonder chiefly about the mind that wrote them down rather than the art he made or failed to make of them. The notebooks, even more than the novels, made Borges think of Kafka and then of Hawthorne, Melville, and Kafka together in a world of "enigmatic punishments and indecipherable sins." Reading Hawthorne's stories, Borges adumbrated his theory of precursors:

> The circumstance, the strange circumstance, of perceiving in a story written by Hawthorne at the beginning of the nineteenth century the same quality that distinguishes the stories Kafka wrote at the beginning of the twentieth must not cause us to forget that Hawthorne's particular quality has been created, or determined, by Kafka. "Wakefield" prefigures Franz Kafka, but Kafka modifies and refines the reading of "Wakefield." The debt is mutual; a great writer creates his precursors. He creates and somehow justifies them.[43]

This conceit makes it possible to read literature without the oppression of history: while we are in this mind, we are as free and as doomed as Borges's Pierre Menard. It is the shortest way out of Salem.

4

Walden

I

It speaks well for American education that children are encouraged to read, from an early age, a book as abrasive as *Walden*, or at least the few charming parts of it—"The Pond in Spring," "Former Inhabitants," and "Spring." Thoreau was not an especially likable man. Emerson spoke of him, at the funeral service, as if he were a phenomenon, a fact of nature rather than of human life. He remarked that his admirers called him "that terrible Thoreau," "as if he spoke when silent, and was still present when he had departed." One of his friends said, according to Emerson: "I love Henry, but I cannot like him; and as for taking his arm, I should as soon think of taking the arm of an elm-tree."[1]

What form the reading of *Walden* takes, in childhood or later, is hard to say. In some schools, I gather, a notional reading of it may allow for soft options, diverting students from the book to a hypothetical camping trip or a parlor game. Kathleen Modenbach, who teaches eleventh-grade American literature in a high school in Alabama, asked her students "to name five items they'd take with them if they were about to set off to live for a year in the woods." The things the youngsters regarded as crucial were "cell phones, make-up, frozen foods, fans, air conditioners, pillows, a car, snack foods, bottled water, toothbrushes, toothpaste, soft drinks, and music." As for the *Walden* they might take with them, it turned out that "my students' anthology included only Sections 16, 19, and 23 of Chapter 2 and parts of the Conclusion."[2] Those few pages would hardly give the students enough cause to acclaim Thoreau as a hero, like the exemplary figure he became in the 1960s.

In 1972 John P. Diggins commented that "among the counterculture and the New Left, [Thoreau] has been resurrected as the patron saint of causes and the guru of cosmic consciousness; to civil rights advocates, the theorist of passive resistance; to militants, the spokesman for direct action; to ecologists, the bachelor of nature; to anarchists, the original 'majority of one'; and to restless students, the inspiring teacher who walked out of the classroom and 'got his head together' to become America's first drop-out."[3] I take Diggins's "resurrected" to mean that before the 1960s Thoreau's presence in American culture was virtual or theoretical: his name was available to allude to many sentiments, but vaguely. Official American culture seems not to have been troubled by the name, so long as its associations remained eccentric or picturesque. Thoreau's being an icon made him a domestic pet. There was no harm in it, no danger, even if it caused people to think that their true lives did not coincide with the conditions in which they lived, or that their lives merely happened to be governed by considerations of money, family, sexual relations, and getting on in the world. There was a recognized risk that their feeling of alienation would increase if they took their discontent seriously, but mostly it was hoped that, given a few years in the bad adult world, they would deal with discontent by occasionally filling up the station wagon with instruments of vacation—tents, gun, fishing rods—and lighting out for mountain or national park. A weekend would be enough. If you felt that Thoreau was watching you, no matter. American culture has always allowed one to feel that there is a "world elsewhere" that is one's true place. It need not be in Kansas. The plenitude of the culture may include the sense of living an adversary life in one's own mind and giving it expression on a few relevant occasions. *Walden* would be a safety valve to keep the engine cool. It might even be regarded as having the expressive status of "The Lake Isle of Innisfree," a poem Yeats wrote under Thoreau's auspices. The poem holds no danger for Irish culture, it presents no social risk, it merely documents one of Yeats's early moods. But *Walden* is more formidable; it holds out the possibility, if only for a year or two, of living a subversive life.

A problem arises, from a civic point of view, only when people put these notions into practice; as those to whom Diggins refers—civil rights advocates, theorists of passive resistance, militants, ecologists, anarchists, and restless students—did in sizable numbers in America in the 1960s. Social theorists became alarmed, belatedly. One of the most eloquent of them, Lionel Trilling, had long anticipated the question he asked himself more urgently when Columbia and other American universities became scenes of conflict among students, faculty, and administration. In a lecture on Freud, given in 1955, Trilling said that Freud "needed to believe that there was some point at which it was possible to stand beyond the reach of culture."[4] But Freud's need did not present an acute problem in 1955. By "culture" Trilling meant a concatenation of social practices having some force in a particular society. In an essay "On the Teaching of Modern Literature" (1961) he asked himself whether by teaching modern literature at Columbia College he bore some responsibility for showing his students that they might stand apart from the general culture and treat it with disdain; a lesson he did not wish them to put into practice. Trilling was willing to see young men and women maintain an intelligent relation to their society, to the degree of irony, but he did not want them to secede from it. The literature he read and taught seemed to him, in one part of his conscience, dangerously attractive in that respect. Reflecting on Thomas Mann's statement that his work could be understood as an effort to free himself from the middle class, Trilling extended the claim beyond the classroom to say that the aim of modern literature "is not merely freedom from the middle class but freedom from society itself":

> I venture to say that the idea of losing oneself up to the point of self-destruction, of surrendering oneself to experience without regard to self-interest or conventional morality, of escaping wholly from the societal bonds, is an "element" somewhere in the mind of every modern person who dares to think of what Arnold in his unaffected Victorian way called "the fullness of spiritual perfection."[5]

Those who want to take their stand outside the general culture make a serious demand on themselves; they insist on achieving under their own volition what Trilling later called authenticity as distinct from the smaller virtue of sincerity. Society, they feel, cannot lead them toward the "undeceived subjectivity" they seek.[6] Trilling believed that a teacher of modern literature must acknowledge these motives as the chief idea and aim of the literature: hence "the striking actuality of our enterprise."[7] The same concern inhabits Trilling's story "Of This Time, Of That Place." The young people whom he instructed how to take modern writing seriously, in a course that included *The Golden Bough, Heart of Darkness, Death in Venice, The Genealogy of Morals, Civilization and Its Discontents, Rameau's Nephew, Notes from Underground,* and "The Death of Ivan Ilyich," may have gone out of the classroom and—some of them—fulfilled the logic of the course by taking over administrative offices, molesting academic deans, and setting bombs to blow up government offices. If they did, they read those books badly. The actions embodied in a work of literature are virtual, not real: they are made to be perceived and to end in the perception. If I murder a king because I have seen a powerful production of *Macbeth,* I have misunderstood the ways of imagination, form, art, and drama. I am invited to imagine what it would be to kill a king, and extend my range of feelings to that extent, but not to act upon the imagining otherwise. I am not, so far as I read literature, a threat to kings or presidents. In my private capacity or as a citizen I may be.

Diggins's list of provocateurs seems to refer to a gone time; his essay is like an evening with the photograph album. Most of the militants who put their theory into practice are dead, in jail, or under trial. Many more have retired to respectability and fame, joined the upper middle class, taken jobs in the university or in Wall Street. Those who are still angry are respected for their anger—Noam Chomsky, Ralph Nader, Mort Sahl—but they have become icons in their turn and are easily enough assimilated to the general culture. It is hard to find a live anarchist or an adept of the once vigorous counterculture. Lawrence Ferlinghetti is a rueful aging poet with a long memory of the good days in San Francisco. The New Left is neither new nor Left. Civil rights activists are involved in disputes about the legality of affirmative action. Students seem to have been pacified; they are worried about finding jobs. That leaves ecologists, who may constitute the only members of a counterculture we have (since rap doesn't apply and Eminem is safe in MTV's bosom). It is possible that President Bush's regime may create a new counterculture in response to his rectitude and depredation.

But American society is gifted in the ways of domestication: it accommodates nearly any force except a foreign force. The normal means of domestication is by turning spiritual values into secular values which can be mistaken for the original impulse. Robert Hughes has remarked of the domestication of Audubon and of Winslow Homer:

> Homer was not, of course, the first "sporting artist" in America, but he was the undisputed master of the genre, and he brought to it both intense observation and a sense of identification with the landscape—just at the cultural moment when the religious Wilderness of the nineteenth century, the church of nature, was shifting into the secular Outdoors, the theater of manly enjoyment. If you want to see Thoreau's America turning into Teddy Roosevelt's, Homer the watercolorist is the man to consult.[8]

There is still a dispute about *Walden*—not about "Civil Disobedience"—and it is conducted mainly by ecologists, whom their opponents call ecocentrists. Ecocentrism did not begin with the publication of Rachel Carson's *Silent Spring* in 1962 or the first Earth Day in 1970. Nor did it end with the publication of Albert

Gore's *Earth in the Balance* (1992). Ecocentrists invoke a tradition of natural history or "nature writing" that includes Walton, Gilbert White, Darwin, Thoreau, Audubon, John Muir, Aldo Leopold, and many writers of our day, notably Annie Dillard and Barry Lopez. Such writers care about the value—not the price—of land. They insist that the world is not our oyster. We are one species among many: we are not entitled to use the natural world as if it were made for our benefit and the exercise of our power. We live on this planet, and we are entitled to survive, but we should live on it as lightly as possible, doing the least possible harm to other forms of life. Thou shalt not kill, beyond the most scrupulous requirements of your staying alive. We should take whatever action we can to address the problems of global warming, ozone depletion, and the accelerating extinction of species. In short: we must change our lives. President George W. Bush is not our patron.

Lawrence Buell, the most spirited ecocentrist in American literary studies, has noted "the tendency among many writers and critics to want to represent the essential America as exurban, green, pastoral, even wild," despite the evidence of cities, slums, industry, commerce, and the drift from rural life. He reveres Thoreau not only for *Walden* and his honorably vigorous essays but for his achieving what Buell calls "the end point in [his] epic of the autonomous self imagining with fascination yet hesitancy the possibility of relinquishing that autonomy to nature."[9] No such imagining ever occurred to Emerson, but it was Thoreau's direction, as it appears to Buell, in the *Journal* after the summer of 1851, when he paid increasing attention to the natural world and less to the nature of his own mind. Sharon Cameron's interests don't coincide with Buell's at every point, but I assume that she, too, subscribes to a version of ecocentrism. Cameron is primarily concerned to show how the *Journal* differs from *Walden,* though her reading of both differs from Buell's. She writes: "*Walden* would produce an account of nature visible for others. The *Journal* turns its back on others in order to maintain: 'There is no interpreter between us and our consciousness' (January 5, 1850 [2:84])." It would not be surprising to find an ideological difference between *Walden* and the *Journal. Walden* was written in several versions over seven years before its publication in August 1854. The *Journal* was written over twenty-four years (from 1837 to 1861) with no evident intention that it should be published. Posterity would decide. The question for an ecocentrist—for any reader, in fact—is why did Thoreau, in the *Journal,* turn his back, if Cameron is right, "on the relation between the social and the natural to explore the relation between the natural and the human—a relation inhospitable to the values and conventions of critical discourse, social by definition?"[10] I think an ecocentrist would have to start farther back by putting all of these putative relations in question. If you want to establish them as relations, you have to work from the ground up, whatever you deem the ground to be, where all the talk begins. Of course no ecocentrist pushes the ideology of green to its theoretical conclusion: you couldn't live if you worried about the feelings of the water you boiled for your coffee or even—

though this is more conceivable—the flowers you cut for the vase on your dinner table.

Anthropocentrists oppose ecocentrists because they regard them as ethically pretentious: no improvement in the ordinary decencies is good enough for them. Anthropocentrists believe that the world was providentially made for man, man being the highest entity in the scale of being, at least thus far, so we are genetically privileged. It would be silly not to enjoy the boon. If you want to live on vegetables or herbs, go ahead, but don't make a metaphysics out of it. Again, it's unlikely that anyone would push his anthropocentrism—or homocentrism, as his opponents call it—to its quasi-logical extreme: at some point you would have to wonder how and why you were deemed superior enough to get away with murder. Those who don't believe that Thoreau was an ecocentrist want to keep him on the anthropocentric side, despite much evidence to the contrary. They do this by maintaining with Leo Marx that *Walden* is a pastoral or a pastoral romance. Marx holds that *Walden* is not what Buell wants it to be:

> Its subject is not the representation of nature "for its own sake"; nor is it primarily a work of nature writing. It is a pastoral, and despite their superficial similarities the two kinds of writing are quite different, in some ways antipathetic. For some two millennia, beginning with the work of two poets of antiquity, Theocritus (third century BC) and Virgil (first century BC), the

> pastoral in literature had portrayed the idealized lives of shepherds, its one constant feature being the contrast, explicit or implied, between their simple ways and the complex worldly lives led by courtiers and city dwellers. Although herdsmen lived in particularly close relations with nature, the literal representation of the nonhuman world rarely if ever had been a part of pastoral.

It follows that "Thoreau was no less interested in society than in nature." Marx makes the point that almost everything Thoreau wrote between 1845 and 1849, "when he conducted his experiment at the pond and spent his night in jail, was informed by an intense awareness of the social and cultural costs of the transition to industrial capitalism."[11]

But "interested," in the sentence I've quoted from Marx about society and nature, darkens the issue. What counts is not the degree of Thoreau's interest but the quality of it. It would be hard to show that Thoreau gave his neighbors in Concord the quality of appreciation, theoretical and practical, he brought to hawk, loon, and water. Marx wants to retain Thoreau for society and politics. He is bound to regard Thoreau's later turn toward quasi-scientific description of the natural world as regrettable, a sign of his loss of nerve and hope, given the damage that industrial capitalism had already done and the further damage it was bent on doing. Marx thinks that Buell and other ecocentrists are misleading about Thoreau; their talk of science and nature writing diverts attention from the only issues that matter, the political conflicts of Thoreau's time and our own. In that respect Marx's best companion could have been William Empson, because Empson's terms of value in *Some Versions of Pastoral* (1935) were political, even though they pointed to a different conclusion. Marx emphasizes in pastoral the "contrast between two ways of life, each grounded in a distinct set of relations with nature."[12] Empson was sensitive to the contrast, and to its origin in different relations with nature, but he found in pastoral a desire to reconcile the rival classes in the end, not to leave them shouting at each other across the fences. "The essential trick of the old pastoral," he says, was "to imply a beautiful relation between rich and poor."[13] Pastoral does not ask us to be blind to social conflicts but to allow ourselves to be brought to a high-minded mood in which they don't seem to matter. As in Gray's "Elegy Written in a Country Churchyard":

> Full many a gem of purest ray serene,
>   The dark unfathomed caves of ocean bear:
> Full many a flower is born to blush unseen,
>   And waste its sweetness on the desert air.

What this means, as Empson says, is that England in the eighteenth century didn't have a scholarship system and therefore wasted the talents of promising boys and girls:

> This is stated as pathetic, but the reader is put into a mood in which one would not try to alter it. (It is true

> that Gray's society, unlike a possible machine society, was necessarily based on manual labour, but it might have used a man of special ability wherever he was born.) By comparing the social arrangement to Nature he makes it seem inevitable, which it was not, and gives it a dignity which was undeserved. Furthermore, a gem does not mind being in a cave and a flower prefers not to be picked; we feel that the man is like the flower, as short-lived, natural, and valuable, and this tricks us into feeling that he is better off without opportunities.[14]

Marx lets the conflicts stand, and thinks only of deploring them: he doesn't remark—as Empson does—how surreptitiously the language of pastoral can appear to take the harm out of them. Buell doesn't see, as Empson does, that an appeal to nature can be made in such a way as to endorse damnable social and political regimes. If the pastoral process is, as Empson shows, one of "putting the complex into the simple," that can be done by implying that the complexities are ultimately extraneous and may be given up in favor of simple and beautiful social relations. Buell's error is to claim that people should commit themselves to nature as other people or the same people also commit themselves to God; but nature, like God, has to be interpreted. The complex thing that Gray does with nature is not allowed for in what Buell does or Buell's Thoreau does.

The dispute between Buell and Marx, as between anthropocentrists and ecocentrists generally, has to be resolved by our deciding not which of them has the better case but which of them has the better claim to Thoreau. It's embarrassing to Buell that Thoreau came to accept the railways and the telegraph, even for the reason that Emerson gave: "In his travels, he used the railroad only to get over so much country as was unimportant to the present purpose."[15] It's embarrassing to Marx that what Thoreau felt for society was mostly sour indifference. I think that ecocentrism and anthropocentrism, though they have held the field of dispute between them for several years, are not especially helpful in our reading of Thoreau. We would do better with a neutral term. His work is autobiography. Not memoir, to invoke a distinction that Jean Starobinski made between these terms. In a memoir, the material is of interest in itself or for historical or cultural reasons; it is, as in Caesar's *Commentaries* and the second part of La Rochefoucauld's *Memoirs*, "narrative which is not distinguished from history by its form." One must learn from external information "that the narrator and the hero are one and the same person." The effacing of the narrator, the objective presentation of the protagonist, "works to the benefit of the event, and only secondarily reflects back upon the personality of the protagonist the glitter of actions in which he has been involved." This is the opposite of pure monologue, "where the accent is on the me and not on the event." In extreme forms of monologue "(not in the domain of autobiography but in that of lyrical fiction), the event is nothing other than the unwinding of the monologue itself, independently of any related 'fact,' which in the process becomes unimportant."[16] In autobiography, the material is of interest (or so I claim) only or mainly because it happened to me, I experienced it. I was the man, I suffered, I was there.

The interest of *Walden* and the *Journal* is that Thoreau's mind was the creative force of each. As he writes in "Where I Lived, and What I Lived For":

> I do not wish to be any more busy with my hands than is necessary. My head is hands and feet. I feel all my best faculties concentrated in it. My instinct tells me that my head is an organ for burrowing, as some creatures use their snout and fore-paws, and with it I would mine and burrow my way through these hills. I think that the richest vein is somewhere hereabouts; so by the divining rod and thin rising vapors I judge; and here I will begin to mine.[17]

It is congenial to Thoreau that "mine" is both a verb and a possessive adjective; the word speaks to what he is and what he lays claim to doing. In the scheme of Northrop Frye's *Anatomy of Criticism* (though at this point Frye is primarily concerned with genres of fiction) *Walden* and the *Journal* would both be called confessions, with allowance made for their incorporating elements of the sermon and of what Frye calls Menippean satire or anatomy, "a vision of the world in terms of a single intellectual pattern," such as melancholy in Burton, fantasy in the Alice books, angling in Walton, erudition (genuine or bogus) in Varro and the Flaubert of *Bouvard et Pecuchet.*[18] The intellectual pattern of *Walden* is Thoreau's sense of the year, the seasons, the habits and repetitions of nature in place and time, but it is his sense, not mine or yours; that is why it is autobiography. The interest never leaves his voice, his pen. Frye notes the mixture of confession and anatomy in *Sartor Resartus,* and it is worth recalling that the remote origin of *Walden* was a lecture that Thoreau gave on Carlyle in the Concord Lyceum on February 4, 1846. Some members of the audience told him that while they were interested in what he said about Carlyle, they would be more interested in anything he would say about himself. On February 10, 1847, he returned to the Lyceum to give a lecture called "A History of Myself." He left Walden Pond on September 6, 1847.

2

If *Walden* and the other books constitute, as I suggest, Thoreau's "song of myself," we need to trace its coordinate terms, beginning with his god-term. Like Emerson, Thoreau tended to speak of God when he had to recognize a fact of life and the world that he could not think of as an effect without a cause. He could not regard the universe as a spontaneous entity without attribution. I am not equating Emerson and Thoreau in this respect. When Emerson gave up his ministry, he retained (as I have claimed) a somewhat more religious sensibility than Thoreau did, short of holding to anything much in the way of a theology. But Thoreau acknowledged a quasi-personal divine power even when he was not required by the argument to do so. In the "Spring" chapter of *Walden* he is merely wondering why one side of a cut on the railway is covered with foliage and the other is not, but "I am affected," he says, "as if in a peculiar sense I stood in the laboratory of the Artist who made the world and me,—had come to where he was still at work, sporting on this bank, and with excess of energy strewing his fresh designs about." In the "Solitude" chapter Thoreau says that "*Next* to us is not the workman whom we have hired, with whom we love so well to talk, but the workman whose work we are." In the "Conclusion," quoting the last verses of Claudian's "De Sene Veronensi"—

> Erret, et extremos alter scrutetur Iberos.
> Plus habet hic vitae, plus habet ille viae—

Thoreau changed Iberos (Spaniards) to "Australians," making the reference more applicable to his own time, and he changed "plus . . . vitae"—"more life"—to "more of God," even at the cost of removing Claudian's play of words between "vitae" and "viae."[19]

But generally Thoreau did not like people enough to give them the dignity of seeming to be a little like the creative God. So he spoke of God, for the most part, as an algebraic value, necessary by definition and to be acknowledged in practice but not otherwise to be commented on. Thoreau assented to God by acknowledging Life and ignoring whatever differences between those values a more strenuous theology would insist on. He managed to do this by thinking of life as a gift from an anonymous donor. Gratuitousness was the quality most to be appreciated: hence, as Sharon Cameron says, "Man is in the natural world as its witness or beholder, not as its explicator."[20] What we witness or behold is life as manifested, which Thoreau—like Emily Dickinson—sometimes called immortality:

> Ah! I have penetrated to those meadows on the morning of many a first spring day, jumping from hummock to hummock, from willow root to willow root, when the wild river valley and the woods were bathed in so pure and bright a light as would have waked the dead, if they had been slumbering in their graves, as some suppose. There needs no stronger proof of immortality. All things must live in such a light. O Death, where was thy sting? O Grave, where was thy victory, then?

The rhetorical claim is not as strong as it is in I Corinthians 15:55: "O death, where is thy sting? O grave, where is thy victory?" Thoreau's exclamations are not universal, they don't go beyond their occasions, but in the next paragraph he chants the occasions so sublimely that the limitation doesn't count: what starts as a simple observation expands its range to end as a neo-Darwinian chorale to life. The paragraph is Thoreau's version of Emerson's "Compensation." Nature, in one of Thoreau's moods as white as moonlight, is here red in tooth and claw, and Thoreau is elated to report that life confounds our moral and sympathetic prejudices:

Our village life would stagnate if it were not for the unexplored forests and meadows which surround it. We need the tonic of wildness,—to wade sometimes in marshes where the bittern and the meadow-hen lurk, and hear the booming of the snipe; to smell the whispering sedge where only some wilder and more solitary fowl builds her nest, and the mink crawls with its belly close to the ground. At the same time that we are earnest to explore and learn all things, we require that all things be mysterious and unexplorable, that land and sea be infinitely wild, unsurveyed and unfathomed by us because unfathomable. We can never have enough of Nature. We must be refreshed by the sight of inexhaustible vigor, vast and Titanic features, the sea-coast with its wrecks, the wilderness with its living and its decaying trees, the thunder cloud, and the rain which lasts three weeks and produces freshets. We need to witness our own limits transgressed, and some life pasturing freely where we never wander. We are cheered when we observe the vulture feeding on the carrion which disgusts and disheartens us and deriving health and strength from the repast. There was a dead horse in the hollow by the path to my house, which compelled me sometimes to go out of my way, especially in the night when the air was heavy, but the assurance it gave me of the strong appetite and inviolable health of Nature was my

> compensation for this. I love to see that Nature is so rife with life that myriads can be afforded to be sacrificed and suffered to prey on one another; that tender organizations can be so serenely squashed out of existence like pulp,—tadpoles which herons gobble up, and tortoises and toads run over in the road; and that sometimes it has rained flesh and blood! With the liability to accident, we must see how little account is to be made of it. The impression made on a wise man is that of universal innocence. Poison is not poisonous after all, nor are any wounds fatal. Compassion is a very untenable ground. It must be expeditious. Its pleadings will not bear to be stereotyped.[21]

Thoreau has Emerson's authority for this, as in the early lecture "School," where Emerson claims that "the laws of disease are the laws of health mashed."[22] Speak for yourself, many readers would say to both sages, and would interrupt Thoreau at "serenely squashed." But the passage is not as brutal as it appears. "Appetite," "health," and "life" are allowed to win, and the negatives ("unexplorable," "unfathomable," "inexhaustible") cut off our desires by pointing to the facts of earthly life, but at least our misgivings are heard in the standard words of their expression, "sacrificed," "suffered," "squashed out of existence," "fatal," and "compassion." In other parts of *Walden,* I agree, Thoreau is content to see "the scale of being" filled and activated by having perch swallow grub-worm, pickerel swallow perch, and fisherman swallow pickerel. Nothing is missing.[23]

Allowing words of protest to be heard, even if then silenced, is the least that Thoreau can do, given that in his terminology God, Life, and Nature are virtually indistinguishable. In Thoreau's trinity, the three are one; but that one is available only to transformed senses. In *A Week on the Concord and Merrimack Rivers* Thoreau rests his oars sufficiently to declare the grounds on which the three are one. He naturalizes God, makes Nature divine such that she is not the symbol of something else but that something itself, and imagines a development of our senses commensurate with the reality they will then apprehend. It is a secular version of the experience of seeing God face to face:

> We need pray for no higher heaven than the pure senses can furnish, a *purely* sensuous life. Our present senses are but the rudiments of what they are destined to become. We are comparatively deaf and dumb and blind, and without smell or taste or feeling. Every generation makes the discovery, that its divine vigor has been dissipated, and each sense and faculty misapplied and debauched. The ears were made, not for such trivial uses as men are wont to suppose, but to hear celestial sounds. The eyes were not made for such groveling uses as they are now put to and worn out by, but to behold beauty now invisible. May we not *see* God? Are we to be put off and

> amused in this life, as it were with a mere allegory? Is not Nature, rightly read, that of which she is commonly taken to be the symbol merely?[24]

"Rightly read" is the problem, if it is our destiny to hear the music of the spheres, see the face of God, and revel in "beauty now invisible."

What then is Nature, if it must be read with this degree of intensity or eked out by human intervention to become divine? Mostly, Thoreau presents it—or her—as Buddha, answering no questions but presenting a comprehensive face:

> After a still winter night I awoke with the impression that some question had been put to me, which I had been endeavouring in vain to answer in my sleep, as what—how—when—where? But there was dawning Nature, in whom all creatures live, looking in at my broad windows with serene and satisfied face, and no question on *her* lips. I awoke to an answered question, to Nature and daylight. The snow lying deep on the earth dotted with young pines, and the very slope of the hill on which my house is placed, seemed to say, Forward! Nature puts no question and answers none which we mortals ask. She has long ago taken her resolution.
> "O Prince, our eyes contemplate with admiration and transmit to the soul the wonderful and varied spectacle

> of this universe. The night veils without doubt a part of this glorious creation; but day comes to reveal to us this great work, which extends from earth even into the plains of the ether."

This would satisfy any prince, provided the terms of the relation were understood as gratuitous: if it is just a matter of beholding, witnessing, and appreciating, without having to ask any questions or answer any. It would also allow Thoreau to feel that the despoiling of forests and rivers doesn't matter, he can be assured—as President Bush is—that they will grow back again, with nothing lost:

> Nevertheless, of all the characters I have known, perhaps Walden wears best, and best preserves its purity. Many men have been likened to it, but few deserve that honor. Though the woodchoppers have laid bare first this shore and then that, and the Irish have built their sties by it, and the railroad has infringed on its border, and the ice-men have skimmed it once, it is itself unchanged, the same water which my youthful eyes fell on; all the change is in me. It has not acquired one permanent wrinkle after all its ripples. It is perennially young, and I may stand and see a swallow dip apparently to pick an insect from its surface as of yore. It struck me again to-night, as if I had not seen it almost daily for more than twenty years,—Why, here is Walden, the

> same woodland lake that I discovered so many years ago; where a forest was cut down last winter another is springing up by its shore as lustily as ever; the same thought is welling up to its surface that was then; it is the same liquid joy and happiness to itself and its Maker, ay, and it *may* be to me.[25]

The only reason I can think of why Thoreau would say something as untrue as this—"unchanged," "the same," "as of yore"—is that the logic of his suppressing the differences between God, Nature, and Life requires him to believe that nature is, like God, invulnerable: nothing that you or I can do to God troubles His security, nor is He bound to offer answers, excuses, or apologies. As in "The Dispersion of Seeds," Thoreau could apply himself to the phenomena, the things on the grounds, trying to make sense of their habits. He was at his best when he paid attention to birds, beasts, flowers, water, and soil rather than to himself in the act of paying such attention.

But there were moments in which Thoreau doubted that Nature was enough, or that it would conduct a wooing both ways between his interests and hers. As in the *Journal* for November 13, 1851:

> Truly a hard day—hard Times these. Not a mosquito left. Not an insect to hum. Crickets gone into winter quarters—Friends long since gone there—& you left to

> walk on frozen ground—with your hands in your pockets. Ah but is not this a glorious time for your deep inward fires?—& will not your green hickory & white oak burn clean—in this frosty air?
>
> Now is not your manhood taxed by the great Assessor? Taxed for having a soul—a rateable soul. A day when you cannot pluck a flower—cannot dig a parsnip nor pull a turnip for the frozen ground—what do the thoughts find to live on? What avails you now the fire you stole from heaven? Does not each thought become a vulture to gnaw your vitals? No Indian summer have we had this November—I see but few traces of the perennial spring.
>
> Now is there nothing—not even the cold beauty of ice crystals—& snowy architecture. Nothing but the echo of your steps over the frozen ground no voice of birds—nor frogs—You are dry as a farrow? Cow. The earth will not admit a spade. All fields lie fallow—Shall not your mind?[26]

In American literature, one answer to the question—"What do the thoughts find to live on?"—is "They live on themselves and on one another." This is Stevens's answer, however provisional, in "The Snow Man": "One must have a mind of winter . . . " If you have a mind of winter, you can survive every moment of blankness, you can even turn nothingness into an affirmative entity:

For the listener, who listens in the snow,
And, nothing himself, beholds
Nothing that is not there and the nothing that is.[27]

But Thoreau, at least in this journal entry, needs crickets, parsnips, and turnips to keep the thinking going. The irony he turns upon "your deep inward fires" is sufficiently appalled to mock Prometheus's act in stealing fire from the gods and giving it to mankind. The eagle, sent to punish Prometheus every day by devouring his liver, becomes in Thoreau's parable the mind itself, endlessly but speciously inventive. The liver that regenerates itself every night to make the punishment eternal is the certainty that one unmoored thought, without turnips, leads only to another. A mind of winter is no satisfaction.

Empson has remarked that there are three main ideas about Nature, "putting her above, equal to, and below man." The three amount to this: (1) "she is the work of God, or a god herself, and therefore a source of revelation," or (2) "she fits man, sympathises with him, corresponds to his social order, has magical connections with him and so forth," or (3) "she is not morally responsible so that to contemplate her is a source of relief (this last is Cowper's main business with her, for example)."[28] Thoreau has something of the three in his sensibility, though he plays down the God of (1). He rarely goes Wordsworthian with (2), but you can find instances of it in the *Journal:* "If I have no friend—what is nature to me? She ceases to be morally significant."[29] He has a lot of (3), which explains why he gets tired of being ecocentrically pious and likes finding life gratuitous without pestering it for disclosures. He is not dismayed to think that Nature has no interest in him. In *Cape Cod* (my favorite among Thoreau's books) he writes: "There is naked Nature,—inhumanly sincere, wasting no thought on man, nibbling at the cliffy shore where gulls wheel amid the spray."[30] A mild version of (1) comes up when he acknowledges that someone we may as well call God must have created a world as wonderful as this one, but Thoreau doesn't want to be always on his knees thanking Him. By identifying God, Nature, and Life, he can spend his life enjoying the spectacle without being precise about its cause.

This is one of the many differences between Thoreau and Gerard Manley Hopkins. Hopkins believed, with as much certainty as that two and three make five, that God created the universe and gave us the privilege of enjoying it and adoring Him. You could do that by praying and by receiving the sacraments of the Roman Catholic Church. You could add to these devotions by paying attention to the created world, the first and most visible book of revelation. If you lavished attention on the world in its multitudinous detail, you practiced something analogous to prayer, if not prayer itself. It was like meditating on a text of the Bible before going on a retreat. Others in Hopkins's day who paid attention to the natural world—Thoreau, Darwin, Chambers, Edward Tuckerman, Hugh Miller, Ruskin, Agassiz—had not Hopkins's clarity of motive, but they had a subdued version of it, attendant on the prestige of the scientific vocation. Empson has pointed out, in an essay on the Alice books, that one reason for the moral grandeur of the Knight is "that he stands for the Victorian scientist, who was felt to have invented a new kind of Roman virtue; earnestly, patiently, carefully (it annoyed Samuel Butler to have these words used so continually about scientists) without sensuality, without self-seeking, without claiming any but a fragment of knowledge, he goes on labouring at his absurd but fruitful conceptions."[31] You would have to feel some of that Roman virtue in yourself before you would think of spending years peering into a pond and annotating what you saw. Thoreau justified it by saying that he had to learn all the laws of Nature if he wanted to understand the harmony of the system:

> If we knew all the laws of Nature, we should need only one fact, or the description of one actual phenomenon, to infer all the particular results at that point. Now we know only a few laws, and our result is vitiated, not, of course, by any confusion or irregularity in Nature, but by our ignorance of essential elements in the calculation. Our notions of law and harmony are commonly confined to those instances which we detect; but the harmony which results from a far greater number of seemingly conflicting, but really concurring, laws, which we have not detected, is still more wonderful.[32]

The one form of nature that Thoreau did not extol, except in ideal or theoretical terms, was the human variety. When he said that "Nature is hard to be overcome, but she must be overcome," he meant human nature.[33] Like Emerson, he did not go in much for sympathy: when he felt himself yielding to that sentiment, he blamed nature, which in one of its aspects he regarded as a soft touch:

> When I have been confined to my chamber for the greater part of several days by some employment or perchance by the ague—till I felt weary & house-worn—I have been conscious of a certain softness to which I am otherwise & commonly a stranger—in which the gates were loosened to some emotions—And if I were to become a confirmed invalid I see how some sympathy with mankind & society might spring up. Yet what is my softness good for even to tears—It is not I but nature in me.[34]

The unforgettable description in *Cape Cod* of the wreck of the Irish famine ship and the remnants of it at Cohasset—Robert Lowell remembered it when he wrote "The Quaker Graveyard in Nantucket"—gets its power from sympathy approached but fended off, such that the details seem like those of a coroner's report: "I saw many marble feet and matted heads as the cloths were raised, and one livid, swollen, and mangled body of a drowned girl,—who probably had intended to go out to service in some American family,—to which some rags still adhered, with a string, half concealed by the flesh, about its swollen neck."[35] In *Walden* Thoreau had not a word of sympathy for James Collins and his family, miserably poor Irish emigrants, to whom he paid four dollars and twenty-five cents for their shack on condition that they vacated it by five o'clock the following morning. Instead, he wrote essays on friendship and love, sublime emotions in principle but not to be looked for in the world or, it appears, regularly practiced there. In *A Week on the Concord and Merrimack Rivers* he made light of both sentiments, claiming that "what is commonly honored with the name of Friendship is no very profound or powerful instinct. . . . Men do not, after all, *love* their Friends greatly."[36] Especially after his rift with Emerson in the summer of 1849, Thoreau gave up expecting much from a friendship and usually anticipated that it would prove disappointing. He felt friendship mostly when the friend was absent or when the glow persisted only in the memory of it. In the *Journal* for April 11, 1852, he wrote: "If I am too cold for human friendship—I trust I shall not soon be too cold for natural influences. It appears to be a law that you cannot have a deep sympathy with both man & nature. Those qualities which bring you near to the one estrange you from the other."[37] He normally associated friendship with feigning, coldness, estrangement, and treachery; and he completed the logic of this prejudice by hating societies, institutions,—"dirty institutions"—the state, the Church, colleges, the medical profession, civilization, philanthropy. "In short, as a snow-drift is formed where there is a lull in the wind, so, one would say, where there is a lull of truth, an institution springs up."[38] He seems even to have despised in his Lyceum audiences the conventions of speech that made it possible for him to address them. In "Natural History of Massachusetts" he said: "In society you will not find health, but in nature. Unless our feet at least stood in the midst of nature, all our faces would be pale and livid. Society is always diseased, and the best is the most so."[39] He had good words for Native American tribes, but not for people who came together in towns and cities.

The only human value that Thoreau acknowledged was the Emersonian one of individuality. He had various words for it: consciousness, mind, spirit, genius, the poet. "No man ever followed his genius till it misled him." "Follow your genius closely enough, and it will not fail to show you a fresh prospect every hour." In the "Conclusion" to *Walden* he has this debonair passage:

> It is said that Mirabeau took to highway robbery "to ascertain what degree of resolution was necessary in order to place one's self in formal opposition to the most sacred laws of society." He declared that "a soldier who fights in the ranks does not require half so much courage as a foot-pad,"—"that honor and religion have never stood in the way of a well-considered and a firm resolve." This was manly, as the world goes; and yet it was idle, if not desperate. A saner man would have found himself often enough "in formal opposition" to what are deemed "the most sacred laws of society,"

> through obedience to yet more sacred laws, and so have tested his resolution without going out of his way. It is not for a man to put himself in such an attitude to society, but to maintain himself in whatever attitude he find himself through obedience to the laws of his being, which will never be one of opposition to a just government, if he should chance to meet with such.[40]

How those laws of one's being are decreed, neither Thoreau nor Emerson ever quite said. It is strange that societies are corrupt while I am pure and my genius unerring. But to be fair to Thoreau and Emerson, you have to start somewhere, with an axiom you take on trust, even if the trust is merely a psychological supposition.

The quality that Thoreau revered in one's genius was its power to imagine further forms of itself and to stand aside from one's mundane or socially imposed interests:

> With thinking we may be beside ourselves in a sane sense. By a conscious effort of the mind we can stand aloof from actions and their consequences; and all things, good and bad, go by us like a torrent. We are not wholly involved in Nature. I may be either the driftwood in the stream, or Indra in the sky looking down on it. I *may* be affected by a theatrical exhibition; on the other hand, I *may not* be affected by an actual event which appears to concern me much more. I only know myself

> as a human entity; the scene, so to speak, of thoughts and affections; and am sensible of a certain doubleness by which I can stand as remote from myself as from another.[41]

But in Thoreau this is not the dramatic or Shakespearean imagination which conceives of forms of existence utterly different from one's own. Thoreau did not write *Hamlet.* He could be a spectator of himself or even a critic, so the sense of doubleness was genuine, as it is in anyone with a conscience. But Thoreau's self was incorrigibly the sovereign self, so well grounded in its values and prejudices that it could attract into its orbit whatever objects and events it paid attention to. In much the same way, Emerson was able to move from the early "Nature" (1836) in which Nature is "the NOT ME" to "The American Scholar" (1837) in which Nature is "the world—this shadow of the soul, or *other me* [which] lies wide around."[42] Such a self is, in Joseph Dunne's description, "a citadel in which a lucid reason is at the service of a naked will."[43]

It is not clear that the sovereign self in Thoreau leads to a distinct philosophy, whether it finds its origin in Descartes or in Hobbes: its relation to Idealism is as close as it comes to being a system. Stanley Cavell has argued that Emerson and Thoreau are philosophers just as Plato and Kant are, but it seems to me better to think of them as sages loosely affiliated to one philosophic tradition or another, mostly Idealism. In *Walden* Thoreau defined philosophy as "economy of living."[44] Neither Emerson nor Thoreau likes to argue a case or defend a position against opponents. Their common styles are aphoristic, suggestive, flinging out an idea and moving on to another one, inspiring or not. "The Brahman never proposes courageously to assault evil, but patiently to starve it out."[45] That sentence is typical of Thoreau in one of his favorite quasi-philosophic styles: it is assertive, it depends on two oppositions—courageously/patiently and assault/starve it out—and it incites further thought about the ways of life it refers to. It is not self-consciously elegant, but it is elegant. It is sage.

Thoreau is never more at one with himself than when he relaxes into the mood he thinks of as Oriental and recommends the *Bhagavad-Gita* as a contemplative ideal. In this mood he becomes not a truculent New Englander but a quietist of Hindu persuasion, as if he had long since brought to a standstill the routines of acrimony, telegrams, and anger. "From the Brahmans," Edward Dahlberg said, "Thoreau learned patience, how to sit and wait, and, so needfully, how to be bored!"[46] He is rarely petulant or fretful, even with his boredom. He usually whiles away the boredom by playing with a word or two, as in this passage he lets his mind drift upon water:

> Thus it appears that the sweltering inhabitants of Charleston and New Orleans, of Madras and Bombay and Calcutta, drink at my well. In the morning I bathe my intellect in the stupendous and cosmogonal philosophy of the Bhagvat Geeta, since whose composition

> years of the gods have elapsed, and in comparison with which our modern world and its literature seem puny and trivial; and I doubt if that philosophy is not to be referred to a previous state of existence, so remote is its sublimity from our conceptions. I lay down the book and go to my well for water, and lo! there I meet the servant of the Brahmin, priest of Brahma and Vishnu and Indra, who still sits in his temple on the Ganges reading the Vedas, or dwells at the root of a tree with his crust and water jug. I meet his servant come to draw water for his master, and our buckets as it were grate together in the same well. The pure Walden water is mingled with the sacred water of the Ganges. With favoring winds it is wafted past the site of the fabulous islands of Atlantis and the Hesperides, makes the periplus of Hanno, and, floating by Ternate and Tidore and the mouth of the Persian Gulf, melts in the tropic gales of the Indian seas, and is landed in ports of which Alexander only heard the names.[47]

Perhaps it is enough to say that this is beautiful and to reflect that most of our lives are niggardly in the allowance they permit to such moments. The sense that the life of water is an archetype of life in general rather than a local constituent of it is not safely removed from decadence, but Thoreau knows that. It is a risk of bad taste he is ready to take. "The pure Walden water" is not an irony, given what he has already said of it; it is a conceit ready to spill over into the sacred water of the Ganges. And the caressing poetry of names with which the passage ends is a permissible swoon, not ordinarily to be indulged except this once.

Thoreau did not argue for such poetry. Generally, he claimed to be writing in the plain style: say what you have to say and finish with it, don't turn somersaults. Make your words your deeds, as Raleigh did.[48] But this is misleading. At least once, in the *Journal,* Thoreau gave a more accurate account of his literary procedures. "Those sentences are good and well discharged," he said, "which are like so many little resiliencies from the spring floor of our lives."[49] But he achieved those resiliencies not from life but from words, and he held himself free to leap to catch any verbal possibility that offered. Most of them arose from the swift transference of a verb or a noun from one context to another. If mortar on bricks is said to grow harder with time, the saying can be said to grow harder with time. If Thoreau doesn't get a stiff neck from using bricks as his pillow, it is because "my stiff neck is of older date."[50] By leaping from nature to culture and back again, Thoreau gained that rapidity of style for which he is admired or, sometimes, resented. Starobinski has remarked that "every original aspect of style implies a redundancy that may disturb the message itself."[51] Even if we think that "the message" is not detachable from the style, the question of redundancy still arises. Starobinski mentions that readers of Rousseau and Chateaubriand often feel that the perfection of their styles contaminates the report of the events they narrate. Thoreau gets most of his resiliencies from sources that some readers deplore, puns and wordplay: pastoral/past; hen-harriers/men-harriers; "A man sits as many risks as he runs"; shore/shorn; grossest/groceries; tripped/traps; aliment/ailment; parlors/parlaver; "It fairly overcame my Nervii"; frontiers/fronts/fronting; sound/sounding/resounding; Quoil/coil; Thor/thaw; "decent weeds, at least, which widowed Nature wears." Not all of these are worth the attention they draw to themselves. I have heard sharper puns from Christopher Ricks in conversation and read more of them in his book on Beckett.

But the extended pun or conceit is Thoreau's favorite device for getting from one sentence to the next. He loves the excess of it because excess is a mark of language itself, never obedient to mere need; as in the "Where I Lived, and What I Lived For" chapter of *Walden.* In this passage the play is on "sleepers," as if he were recalling the last sentence of *Wuthering Heights,* in which Lockwood wonders "how anyone could ever imagine unquiet slumbers, for the sleepers in that quiet earth."[52] Sleepers are pieces of timber on which sections of a railway are laid. They are also people asleep or, as in Lockwood's mind, people dead. On the railway each piece of timber is cut exactly to the same length, breadth, and thickness as the other ones. The spaces between them are the same and they are laid in parallel lines. Sleepers in bed and the grave are also prone. In sound sleep the differences between one person and another are reduced. When you read Whitman's "The Sleepers," you must not think of railways: when you read *Walden* you must, and you must also stay awake to be switched from railway to bed or grave and back again. In "House-Warming" Thoreau, roaming "the then boundless chestnut woods of Lincoln," says: "They now sleep their long sleep under the railroad." In "Where I Lived, and What I Lived For" he has been talking about morning, the merit of being awake, the need to simplify our lives:

> Men think that it is essential that the *Nation* have commerce, and export ice, and talk through a telegraph, and ride thirty miles an hour, without a doubt, whether *they* do or not; but whether we should live like baboons or like men, is a little uncertain. If we do not get out sleepers, and forge rails, and devote days and nights to the work, but go to tinkering upon our *lives* to improve *them,* who will build railroads? And if railroads are not built, how shall we get to heaven in season? But if we stay at home and mind our business, who will want railroads? We do not ride on the railroad; it rides upon us. Did you ever think what those sleepers are that underlie the railroad? Each one is a man, an Irishman, or a Yankee man. The rails are laid on them, and they are covered with sand, and the cars run smoothly over them. They are sound sleepers, I assure you. And every few years a new lot is laid down and run over; so that, if some have the pleasure of riding on a rail, others have the misfortune to be ridden upon. And when they run over a man

> that is walking in his sleep, a supernumerary sleeper in the wrong position, and wake him up, they suddenly stop the cars, and make a hue and cry about it, as if this were an exception. I am glad to know that it takes a gang of men for every five miles to keep the sleepers down and level in their beds as it is, for this is a sign that they may sometime get up again.[53]

The conceit nearly runs away from itself with the man walking in his sleep, "a supernumerary sleeper in the wrong position." Thoreau's imagination is promiscuous, but he has the excuse that the English and the American languages are also promiscuous: such a word as *sleeper* should make a space for itself and keep out foreigners, but it doesn't, it doesn't defend itself against the other *sleeper* and *underlie* and *beds* and the bizarre image of wooden sleepers turning into human sleepers and dying for the privilege. When Thoreau comes to a Coleridgean choice between Imagination and Understanding, he does not hesitate:

> The fable which is naturally and truly composed, so as to satisfy the imagination, ere it addresses the understanding, beautiful though strange as a wild-flower, is to the wise man an apothegm, and admits of his most generous interpretation. When we read that Bacchus made the Tyrrhenian mariners mad, so that they leapt into the sea, mistaking it for a meadow full of flowers, and so became dolphins, we are not concerned about the

> historical truth of this, but rather a higher poetical truth. We seem to hear the music of a thought, and care not if the understanding be not gratified.[54]

In literary work of the greatest power there is no need to adjudicate between imagination and understanding, each has its rights, but Thoreau doesn't come into that supreme reckoning. His distinction is in the music of a thought and the music of what further happens.

The merit of saying that Thoreau is primarily an autobiographer is that it guards him against being kidnapped. The people whom Diggins referred to—the several groups—kidnapped Thoreau each for his or her cause. More recently, the ecocentrists have tried to take him over, or make him over. Autobiography is not a cause, except that it is a cause of wonder that people as strange as Augustine, Montaigne, Rousseau, and Thoreau should exist.

5

Leaves of Grass

I

Wallace Stevens's poem "Like Decorations in a Nigger Cemetery" begins:

> In the far South the sun of autumn is passing
> Like Walt Whitman walking along a ruddy shore.
> He is singing and chanting the things that are part of him,
> The worlds that were and will be, death and day.
> Nothing is final, he chants. No man shall see the end.
> His beard is of fire and his staff is a leaping flame.[1]

Usually, a poet's recourse to a mythic perspective starts with a human agent and then lifts his eyes to the stars or to a divine figure from the lore of Greece, Egypt, Rome, or India. In "The Idea of Order at Key West" the singing woman "sang beyond the genius of the sea," and in "The Comedian as the Letter C" Crispin is presented in relation to "the legendary moonlight" that once burned in his mind. Sea and moonlight are brought to bear upon the woman and Crispin, with whatever consequences we interpret the relations as effecting. It is unusual to have the sun come first and then be compared to a poet walking along the beach. Only a name of mythic grandeur could sustain the simile. "Like Decorations in a Nigger Cemetery" continues for forty-nine more stanzas, most of them only three lines long but a few of them four or five, no stanza having any particular bearing on Whitman or on the kind of poetry he wrote, except for stanza 47, which starts: "The sun is seeking something bright to shine on." The Whitman invoked there is probably the "I, chanter of pains and joys, uniter of here and hereafter" of "Out of the Cradle Endlessly Rocking." But the allusion is casual. Each stanza muses, apparently, on the litter of anything Stevens feels inclined to muse on, including the character of poetry:

> Poetry is a finikin thing of air
> That lives uncertainly and not for long
> Yet radiantly beyond much lustier blurs.[2]

The point of the first stanza may be to say: "Whitman is the kind of poet an American Romantic poet is expected to be, and these are the grand gestures he is expected to make. I don't despise their grandeur. Indeed, I have done some seaside chanting myself in two or three poems and may do so again, but I am now inclined to attempt something different: gnomic, unforthcoming, as arbitrary as Cubism." In fact, Stevens did not much care for Whitman's poems. In a letter of February 8, 1955, to Joseph Bennett, he wrote of Whitman in the nerveless style he reserved for letters he would prefer not to have to write:

> I can well believe that he remains highly vital for many people. The poems in which he collects large numbers of concrete things, particularly things each of which is poetic in itself or as part of the collection, have a validity which, for many people, must be enough and must seem to them all opulence and élan.
>
> For others, I imagine that what was once opulent begins to look a little threadbare and the collections seem substitutes for opulence even though they remain gatherings-together of precious Americana, certain to remain precious but not certain to remain poetry. The typical élan survives in many things.
>
> It seems to me, then, that Whitman is disintegrating as the world, of which he made himself a part, disintegrates. "Crossing Brooklyn Ferry" exhibits this disintegration.
>
> The élan of the essential Whitman is still deeply moving in the things in which he was himself deeply moved. These would have to be picked out from compilations like "Song of the Broad-Axe," "Song of the Exposition."

> It is useless to treat everything in Whitman as of equal merit. A great deal of it exhibits little or none of his specific power. He seems often to have driven himself to write like himself. The good things, the superbly beautiful and moving things, are those that he wrote naturally, with an extemporaneous and irrepressible vehemence of emotion.[3]

The stanza about Whitman in "Like Decorations in a Nigger Cemetery" seems mainly to indicate that Whitman, whatever he is for Stevens, has become for many American readers a myth, heroic archetype of a late-Romantic poet, according to a tradition from which Stevens would propose, at least for the moment, to distance himself. If we doubt Whitman's mythic status in American culture, we have only to insert another name (making any necessary grammatical adjustments) to see the stanza collapse. Try inserting the name of Whittier, Bryant, Emerson, Longfellow, Dickinson, Pound, Hart Crane, Frost, Eliot, Robert Lowell, or John Ashbery. Crane might hold the lines intact, his myth being like Whitman's in kind if not in scale; but just barely. Any other name would humiliate the stanza.

The problem is: how to cope with a myth. A mythic figure in literature is someone who in common opinion is thought to exceed his works and may be deemed, as a personality, to replace them. A golden penumbra surrounds his name, even for people who have given up reading his books or stopped short of reading them. Keats is whatever penumbra surrounds his name. The main difficulty with Whitman is not the desirability of removing him from some mythic Mount Rushmore: it is rather how to read *Leaves of Grass* without first taking a position on several other issues that demand one's attention for extraneous reasons: America ("These States"), democracy ("I shall use the words America and democracy as convertible terms"[4]), versions of love ("amativeness," love of man and woman, "adhesiveness," love of man and man), and death ("the word stronger and more delicious than any," according to "Out of the Cradle Endlessly Rocking"). Only then, having cleared some of the ground, is it possible to read the poems as if they were poems rather than national anthems, hymns, manifestos, or campaign speeches. The ground being cleared, I find especially telling "Song of Myself," "Crossing Brooklyn Ferry," "Whoever You Are Now Holding Me in Hand," "Out of the Cradle Endlessly Rocking," "As I Ebb'd with the Ocean of Life," "Tears," "On the Beach at Night," "Vigil Strange I Kept on the Field One Night," "Reconciliation," "Lo, Victress on the Peaks," "When Lilacs Last in the Dooryard Bloomed," "There Was a Child Went Forth," "The Sleepers," "The Dalliance of the Eagles," and "Give Me the Splendid Silent Sun." In many other passages of verse and prose, what you think of Whitman's claims—"The United States themselves are essentially the greatest poem" and other hyperboles—intimidates you as you turn the pages.[5] Annotation is not the answer. Few of Whitman's poems need footnotes in the sense in which first readers of Yeats's "The Second Coming" need to be told what he meant by "*spiritus mundi.*" To read Whitman's "O Star of France," the only bit of information you need is that the Franco-Prussian War ended in 1871 with the defeat of France. The problem of reading *Leaves of Grass* is in coming to terms with Whitman not merely as the author of certain poems but as a phenomenon, portentous indeed, of American culture.

Not that there is an agreed position on this score. I'll try to convey some sense of a context of debate that seems constructive and is in any case unavoidable. This entails postponing a consideration of the poems, but I don't see any way of coming to them immediately unless I ignore the public issues in which Whitman is evidently a presence. Democracy is the first of these, and may represent other issues, whether by democracy Whitman means representative government consistent with certain rights and duties, or a more comprehensive value hard to distinguish from his ideas of religion, morality, or universal love. Some readers hold with Thoreau that Whitman was "apparently the greatest democrat the world has ever seen." Readers less given to superlatives apparently agree with F. O. Matthiessen that Whitman was a democrat of socialist conviction who "possessed none of the power of thought or form that would have been necessary to give his poems of ideal democracy any perfection, and to keep them from the barrenness of abstraction."[6] But it is evidently enough that he proclaimed the supreme merit of democracy, whatever he meant. He was not a Marxist: no revolutionary zeal propels his feeling for the proletariat.

But the argument about Whitman's sensibility becomes more pointed when it is recovered from Santayana's *Interpretations of Poetry and Religion* and *The Last Puritan.* In the *Interpretations* Santayana presented Whitman and Browning as exemplars of "the poetry of barbarism":

> The barbarian is the man who regards his passions as their own excuse for being; who does not domesticate them either by understanding their cause or by conceiving their ideal goal. He is the man who does not know his derivations nor perceive his tendencies, but who merely feels and acts, valuing in his life its force and its filling, but being careless of its purpose and its form. His delight is in abundance and vehemence; his art, like his life, shows an exclusive respect for quantity and splendour of materials.

Whitman, according to Santayana, has made "the imaginary experiment of beginning the world over again," ignoring "the fatal antiquity of human nature." With Whitman, the surfaces of things are everything, the underlying structure is of no interest. Although he was a democrat, he did not understand democracy as it was or as it might have become: "The literature of democracy was to ignore all extraordinary gifts of genius or virtue, all distinction drawn even from great passions or romantic adventures. In Whitman's works, in which this new literature is foreshadowed, there is accordingly not a single character nor a single story."[7] The absence of character and story from Whitman's poems is, I think, the crucial consideration.

The reason for this is that by assenting to the validity of character and story one accepts the fact that our lives are conditioned, though not determined. My character is a consequence of my birth, my father and mother, social class, money, physical constitution, education, environment. Even if we make a distinction, as Yeats did, between character and personality, as between chance and choice, the choice is not absolute or free of constraint. Story is an acknowledgement of the actuality of our lives and the evident fact of other lives. Magical realism and Romance extend the range of possibility, in deference to one's desire to be free of limits, but in the end these genres assent to the conditions they notionally transcend. Most of the objections to Whitman's poetry are for that reason footnotes to Santayana's. I'll refer to some of them briefly and mainly for their different tones.

R. P. Blackmur retains Santayana's vocabulary while ad libbing among his words to go beyond them. Comparing Whitman with Pound, he writes:

> Each is a barbarian, and neither ever found a subject that compelled him to composition; each remained spontaneous all his life. . . . Nobody ever learned anything but attitude or incentive from Whitman. His example liberates the vatic weakness in others—that easiest of all reservoirs, spontaneity. . . . The barbarians

> are those outside us whom we are tempted to follow when we would escape ourselves. We imitate Whitman to get emotion. . . . Both [Pound and Whitman] are good poets when we ourselves wish to be fragmentary. . . . Whitman is a crackerbarrel *Song of Solomon* proceeding by seizures. But he is also the Bard of everything in us that wants to be let alone so that we can be together, and he knows how to get rid of all the futility of mere meaning and the horror of mere society.[8]

But to other readers that skill of riddance seems insidious. Quentin Anderson has argued that *Leaves of Grass,* however gratifying it appears, is really an attack on the whole structure of culture, so far as that culture is predicated on history, family, character, story, and accident. Far from sustaining the world or helping us to endure it, the poems dissolve it, because nothing in the world is allowed to offer any resistance to Whitman's consciousness of it. Whitman feels especially threatened by the authority of anyone else's mind:

> Much of Whitman's poetry has a bland, unspoken, yet terrible violence toward other human existence. When we think of the multitude of passengers crossing Brooklyn Ferry, a march of the generations, and of the violence involved in the assertion that all are to *see the same thing;* that no one is to be permitted to color that scene to the shape of his intention or interest, we begin to get a

> glimpse of the enormous cancellations we have so often gladly accepted at Whitman's hands.

It follows, according to Anderson, that "if we want freedom we must find it in the complex relationships of the outer world; Whitman can only be associated with 'democracy' at the price of making the term meaningless."[9]

But the most far-reaching attack on Whitman's poetry was made by Yvor Winters. In an essay on his one-time friend Hart Crane, Winters maintained that Crane got his ideas, jejune as they were, from Whitman, who got them from Emerson, a deplorable source. "The doctrine of Emerson and Whitman, if really put into practice, should naturally lead to suicide," to Crane's suicide, specifically: "In the first place, if the impulses are indulged systematically and passionately, they can lead only to madness; in the second place, death, according to the doctrine, is not only a release from suffering but is also and inevitably the way to beatitude. . . . There is no question, according to the doctrine, of moral preparation for salvation; death leads automatically to salvation." Commenting on Pocahontas in the poems of Crane's "Powhatan's Daughter," Winters wrote:

> [He] is the symbol of the American soil, and the five poems deal more or less clearly with the awakening love of the young protagonist for his country and for the deity with which his country is identified. We have here a characteristically Whitmanian variation on Emerson's

> pantheism: for Emerson God and the universe were one, but for Whitman the American soil was the part of the universe to be especially worshipped, so that the pantheistic mysticism tends to become a national mysticism.[10]

Winters's main criticism of Crane, Whitman, and Emerson was that they were not interested in understanding or assessing their feelings; it was enough for them that they had feelings and, at least by their own estimate, had them in abundance. The difference in quality between one feeling and another was of no account. We come back to Santayana or, a few years later, to Pound, who complained in *The Spirit of Romance* of "that horrible air of rectitude with which Whitman rejoices in being Whitman."[11] (But Pound veered on Whitman, and often spoke well of him.) Many of these criticisms argue that Whitman listened, readily and without irony, to what Eliot called—though he did not mention Whitman on the occasion—the Whiggery of the Inner Voice.[12]

2

It may be possible to deflect the force of these criticisms somewhat (though hardly to remove them). The readers I have quoted, from Santayana to Anderson, assume that in all his poems Whitman is speaking on his own authority, or the appropriated authority of Emerson. When he says "I" he means "I, my empirical, historical, psychological self." But it is necessary to distinguish at least three figures who go under the same name. The first is the historical

Walter Whitman, who held jobs as newspaperman, editor, and writer, nursed soldiers in the Civil War, lived and died. In those capacities he coincides with himself in a life fairly commonplace. The second figure is the poet Walt Whitman, who invented himself as seer and prophet. He does not coincide with the first except betimes. Walter Whitman was never in California or in Platte Canyon; he did not witness the execution of John Brown. He was not born in Kentucky, as "O Magnet-South" implies.[13] Walt Whitman imagined for himself a life beyond the life he lived, and wrote the imagining. The source of his vision was the language he read and spoke—English, American, with fragments of Spanish and French thrown in for cosmopolitan effect. The third figure may be called Whitman, it has no other name, nor is it found among its ostensible manifestations: it is the Emersonian force of spirit or *pneuma,* the wind that bloweth where it listeth. It is the genius—whether the *genius loci* or some other irregular formulation—that made Whitman possible without exhausting its powers in doing so.

Of these three: the first is matter for a biographer, the third can be invoked, but invocation is nearly all that can be done with it; the second is more tangible. When I say that Walter Whitman invented himself as the poet Walt Whitman, I don't mean that he produced a character as in a play, *Hamlet, King Lear,* or *Murder in the Cathedral.* It would be better to think of Yeats's invention of Michael Robartes and Crazy Jane, Rilke's invention of Malte Laurids Brigge, Eliot's invention of J. Alfred Prufrock and Gerontion. In these cases we are not meant to imagine people, or dramatic characters, semblances of fully embodied agents carrying out actions on their own responsibility in a world of other agents and antagonists. Each of these inventions by Yeats, Rilke, and Eliot is a mood or a gesture, isolated for sustained attention, articulated for the occasion but not meant to live beyond it. "J. Alfred Prufrock is a name plus a Voice," Hugh Kenner has maintained.[14] Donald Davie argued that we are not to take Gerontion as a person "but only a *persona*—he is given a phantasmal life only provisionally, not fully bodied forth."[15] Gerontion—a shade, not a person—enables certain feelings to be expressed without having them attributed to anyone in particular; though readers can't be prevented from judging the feelings as if they were specifically someone's or their own. In "Byzantium" Yeats writes:

> Before me floats an image, man or shade,
> Shade more than man, more image than a shade.[16]

The ascendancy of image over shade and of shade over man makes it impossible for readers to settle for any one of the three as definitive or for a possible fourth that would be more complete than any of the three. So, I think, with the poet Walt Whitman. In "Salut au Monde!" he names himself, or rather his second self: "What do you hear Walt Whitman?" In "Song of Myself," "I and this mystery here we stand." But mostly the speaker of the poems is given as "I." Not a name plus a voice: just a voice.

Nor is the voice singular: it is generic. Allen Grossman has persuasively argued that the impression of a singular voice can be achieved in poetry only by having an abstract pattern of meter and a speaking will playing off against each other, like competitors without whom there could be no game. The "natural stress characteristics of language" then play against "an abstract and irrational pattern of counted positions," and the consequence is a conviction of identity in the voice.[17] I quote a well-established instance from Wyatt:

They fle from me that sometyme did me seke
With naked fote stalking in my chamber.
I have sene theim gentill tame and meke
That nowe are wyld and do not remember
That sometyme they put theimself in daunger
To take bred at my hand; and nowe they raunge
Besely seeking with a continuell chaunge.

Thancked be fortune, it hath ben othrewise
Twenty tymes better; but ons in speciall
In thyn arraye after a pleasaunt gyse
When her lose gowne from her shoulders did fall,
And she me caught in her armes long and small;
Therewithall swetely did my kysse
And softely said "dere hert, how like you this?"

It was no dreme: I lay brode waking.
But all is torned thorough my gentilnes
Into a straunge fasshion of forsaking;

And I have leve to goo of her goodeness,
And she also to vse new fangilnes.
But syns that I so kyndely ame serued,
I would fain knowe what she hath deserued.[18]

That is a singular voice, as close as print can come to the semblance of a particular man uttering his sense of his experience at court and in the bedroom over a period, it may be, of years. Reading the poem, we are close enough to hear the speaker. We never release ourselves from him, his voice, his sense—from one moment to the next—of living a life bruised, embittered, ironic, superior, passive, aggressive, punitive, erotic, whimpering. He uses the vocabulary of the court ("I have leve," "I would fain knowe," "torned thorough my gentilnes") as if he could not yet give up its values, miserable as they have made him. He also knows what has gone wrong ("new fangilnes") and how empty the old ways ("kyndely") have turned out to be. The poem ends with a hapless question, because the appeal to justice ("deserued") is the most irrelevant one he could make. When all else is broken, he calls for justice as the system of things that should obtain. This is a poem—to use a distinction of Rosemond Tuve's—of "a man having thoughts" rather than of "the thoughts a man had."[19] It is crucial to our appreciating the poem that we feel we are listening to one man and that he is not claiming, at least for now, to be a representative victim. He is not speaking for mankind. For the time being, life is as it impinges upon him and is expressed in a particular voice that moves from one tone to another. The world beyond the court, outside the rooms of complaint and love, might as well not exist. This sense, too, is part of the pressure the poem exerts upon us. We read it as if we were trying to follow, in performance, a difficult piece of music.

Grossman's argument is that Whitman's choice of a poetic line made singularity of voice impossible. Whitman deemed the meters of English verse to be corrupt, as Grossman says, "indelibly stained by the feudal contexts of its most prestigious instances." Besides, the old meters required the suppression of the natural turns of American speech, "and therefore an abridgment of the freedom of the speaker." These meters, the degraded ministry of iambs, trochees, and dactyls, would have denied Whitman access to his theme of freedom. So he repudiated them and settled for "free verse" and "open form." As a result, Grossman says:

> In the chronology of Whitman's work, the "open" line as formal principle appears simultaneously with the subject of liberation, and is the enabling condition of the appearance of that subject. That is to say, his first poems in the new style are also his first poems on the subject of slavery and freedom (specifically, "Resurgemus," "Blood-Money," "Wounded in the House of Friends").

But the price Whitman had to pay for his new style and his fated theme was the loss of singularity. He could say "I" only by claiming that "I feel, and my feeling has the privilege of representing yours."

Even that price turned out to be higher than he could have anticipated. As Grossman notes: "Whitmanian celebration by pluralization extinguishes all personhood which has *only* singular form."[20] Even in the elegy for Lincoln, Whitman finds himself writing:

> Nor for you, for one alone,
> Blossoms and branches green to coffins all I bring,
> For fresh as the morning, thus would I chant a song for
> you O sane and sacred death.[21]

All he could hope to achieve by *vers libre* was an endless apostrophe to "I and Thou" on the basis of the axiomatic transparence of persons, "reciprocal internality, of persons one to the other ('What I shall assume you shall assume')."[22] We have seen that that formulation has been interpreted, notably by Quentin Anderson, as evidence of a totalitarian claim upon the world.

There is also the question: if Whitman's poetic voice must be generic or representative rather than singular, what can it say, what values can it live by? No matter how plural its invocations, the rhetoric of "I, like you, whoever you are," can't be an acknowledgement of differences, it can only be an assertion of the same. It cannot say anything else but: "I take your point, that you and I are not, as things stand, the same. Socially, you are a slave, I am a master. But in spiritual principle and in a future which I prophesy will fulfill that principle, you and I will be the same. So even now there is no need to 'regard the hovels of those that live in this land.'" Those who find *Leaves of Grass,* like many of Emerson's essays, chilling do so for that reason. The book seems to tell the people who live in hovels—in the Appalachian mountains, for example, or the slums of Chicago—that they need not fret; spiritually, they are the same as the people who live in elegant suburbs and wash their Jaguars on Sunday mornings. On this principle, Whitman cannot discriminate between one person and another, one entity and another. If he is to maintain that all things are one and the same, he can only declare what Grossman calls "the goodness of simple presence" as the human axiom, the good of mere being without further tally, "the presence of the person prior to all other characteristics."[23] Whitman, speaking in "By Blue Ontario's Shore" of "the poet," says—repeating the sentiment from the 1855 preface—"He judges not as the judge judges but as the sun falling around a helpless thing."[24] That is: he doesn't judge at all, since the sun falls impartially upon a helpless thing and a thug. It is a rhetoric of parataxis: one thing, then another and another. There must be no preference, privilege, or discrimination of kind or degree. If the value to be celebrated is presence-before-identity, presence-before-difference, it is universal but empty. I would choose it only in preference to being dead. The fact that the line is one of the most beautiful lines in Whitman's poetry is sufficiently explained by its making us want to live in a world in which such a judgment—no judgment at all—would be enough. The price gets higher. If Whitman is to commit himself to a world without difference—we come back again to Santayana's commentary—he must station himself at the point of farthest remove from the "minute particulars" of the world, he must take up the zero degree of vantage where he can see all things reduced to their appearances and those appearances the same. The only difference separates the living from the dead; and even that is not supposed to count. Contrasting Whitman with Lincoln for the moment, Grossman writes of a passage in "When Lilacs Last in the Dooryard Bloom'd"—"I saw battle-corpses, myriads of them,/And the white skeletons of young men, I saw them.":

> Through the establishment of difference between the living and the dead—a laying of ghosts, including Lincoln and his meanings—the elegist recovers the perceptibility of his world, as Lincoln had established the difference between persons and things by the emancipation of the slaves, and this restored the rationality of the polity. But the act of perceptual autonomy ("free sense") finds Whitman, at the moment of his greatest originality, at the greatest distance also from the social world in which alone his intention can have meaning, that world over which Lincoln presided as emancipator, accounting for the same facts of suffering (at Gettysburg, for example, or in the "Second Inaugural") according to compensatory economies of theodicy, those of dedication, sacrifice, and the vengeance of God.

None of these economies is available to Whitman, since they entail one's coming into history and assenting to the social character of life with all its differences and cruelties. Whitman, "the master of social love," as Grossman puts it, "was unable, by the nature of his fundamental revision of personhood, to enter the world by any act, except the deathwatch of the wounded in Lincoln's war."[25]

There is a corresponding difficulty in Whitman's recourse to the grammatical second person and the third. Neither of them can denote a particular entity. Each has purchase only on a referent generic and representative. In *Pragmatism* William James quoted a few stanzas from the 1856 version of "To You," a poem evidently addressed to the reader or hearer of *Leaves of Grass,* whoever he or she may be, and therefore in principle to any "you":

> Whoever you are, now I place my hand upon you, that
>   you be my poem,
> I whisper with my lips close to your ear,
> I have loved many women and men, but I love none
>   better than you.[26]

In the remaining stanzas Whitman claims to know the real You beneath the poses and disfigurements that degrade it. It corresponds to the "Me myself" that Whitman claims to intuit in "Song of Myself." In "To You," "Through angers, losses, ambition, ignorance, ennui, what you are picks its way." James argues that there are two ways of reading the poem, "both useful," though one more useful than the other. The first is "the monistic way, the mystical way of pure cosmic emotion." The glories and grandeurs are already yours absolutely, "even in the midst of your defacements." Whatever happens to you, "inwardly you are safe." "Look back, *lie* back, on your true principle of being!" This is the quietist interpretation: "Its enemies compare it to a spiritual opium." But pragmatism "must respect this way, for it has massive historic vindication." Nevertheless, James's version of pragmatism favors another way of interpreting the poem, the pluralistic way. "The you so glorified, to which the hymn is sung, may mean your better possibilities, phenomenally taken, or the specific redemptive effects even of your failures, upon yourself or others." It may mean "your loyalty to the possibilities of others whom you admire and love so that you are willing to accept your own poor life, for it is that glory's partner." Identify your life with those possibilities, and the real You begins to live. Both of these interpretations, according to James, are valid: "Both sanctify the human flux." Both "paint the portrait of the *you* on a golden background." But the background of the first way is "the static One," while the second way "means possibles in the plural, genuine possibles, and it has all the restlessness of that conception." The first way "takes the world's perfection as a necessary principle," the second takes it "only as a possible *terminus ad quem*." The first finds its perfection *anti rem*, the second *in rebus*.[27] Pragmatism favors the second way because it entails taking one step at a time rather than positing a timeless principle of perfection. But James does not advert to the fact that, in either interpretation, the "you" is not any particular you, it does not grasp particularity or individuality, the "I" is just as distant from "you" as from any other social object. "You" is not distinct from any "him" or "her." Because the "you" is a supreme fiction, "it must be abstract," as Stevens says. Whitman is honest about this. The only destiny the "you" has—once the poet's hand is placed upon "you"—is to "be my poem." Every object returns to be a function of the subject: it is the purest form of idealism which tells entities that they are mere signs.

The third grammatical person suffers the same indignity. No ostensibly external thing in Whitman's poetry coincides with its existence, it is always at a remove from itself—ideal, abstract, hypothetical, at most a promissory note, a type to be fulfilled "in our next." "The real something has yet to be known," as Whitman writes in "Of the Terrible Doubt of Appearances."[28] One of the most gorgeous instances of an ostensibly third person is the section of "Song of Myself" about the twenty-ninth bather:

> Twenty-eight young men bathe by the shore,
> Twenty-eight young men and all so friendly;
> Twenty-eight years of womanly life and all so lonesome.
>
> She owns the fine house by the rise of the bank,
> She hides handsome and richly drest aft the blinds of
>   the window.
> Which of the young men does she like the best?
> Ah the homeliest of them is beautiful to her.
>
> Where are you off to, lady? for I see you,
> You splash in the water there, yet stay stock still in your
>   room.

Dancing and laughing along the beach came the twenty-
ninth bather,
The rest did not see her, but she saw them and loved
them.

The beards of the young men glisten'd with wet, it ran
from their long hair,
Little streams pass'd all over their bodies.

An unseen hand also pass'd over their bodies,
It descended tremblingly from their temples and ribs.

The young men float on their backs, their white bellies
bulge to the sun, they do not ask who seizes fast to
them,
They do not know who puffs and declines with pendant
and bending arch,
They do not think whom they souse with spray.[29]

This genre-painting—Thomas Eakins's "The Swimming Hole" has been suggested as a source—is one of many examples of Whitman's aesthetic of contact. "I will go to the bank by the wood and become undisguised and naked,/I am mad for it to be in contact with me," he writes at the beginning of "Song of Myself." John Hollander has interpreted the passage as "a fable of the moon becoming moonlight in order to make love to the twenty-eight days," and he has associated it with the parable of the harlot in Proverbs 7.[30] The woman sees the young men bathing and enters the water, caressing them. Or rather, the narrator engages in the fantasy by which she does this; and the fantasy has the effect of transforming the woman into himself. She merges with him to become the twenty-ninth bather. There aren't thirty bathers. The woman, the third person, becomes the first person, giving up her differences—social class, money, possessions, maturity, isolation—to merge with the narrator. "You splash in the water there, yet stay stock still in your room." The merging corresponds to—but is not the same as—the orgasms of the twenty-eight men. The "unseen hand" is a composite fantasy of a man and a woman, masturbating the bathers. There is no need to think that Whitman guarded himself against rebuke by presenting a woman rather than a man gazing with desire at the bathers.[31] Even if he did, the poem would still enact the fantasy by which a grammatical third person loses his or her autonomy for the sake of becoming the first person, the poet, master of the occasion.

3

The reduction of third person to first is a risk in the version of "the sublime poem" that Josephine Miles has attributed to Whitman. The main distinction she makes is between poetry based on the clause and poetry based on the phrase. Clausal poetry is logical, or it runs to a show of logical concepts and argument. It entails the direction of energy through main and subordinate clauses, with discriminations, qualifications, assertions and denials: it delights in the play of "if," "therefore," "yet," "because," and "but." The poem by Wyatt I've quoted is clause poetry. Phrasal poetry works more loosely and finds its highest form in the sublime poem. The sublime poem tries not to do its theme justice but to suffuse it, overwhelm it with the poet's passion. Such poetry has "its specific complex of traits: an epithetical, phrasal, participial, and compounding sentence structure, an unrhymed or irregular ode line, a vocabulary of passion and magnitude." Historically, the sublime poem issues from the combined force of the Bible (especially the Psalms), Milton, Fénelon, and Longinus:

> How may the sublime poem be distinguished? First of all, by its cumulative phrasal sentence structure, its piling up of nouns and epithets, participles and compounds, with a very minimum of clausal subordinations and active verbs. Second, by its vocabulary of cosmic passion and sense impression. Third, by its internal rather than external patterning of sound, the interior tonal shadings and onomatopoeias of its unrhymed verse. In combination, these three major traits make for an exceptionally panoramic and panegyric verse, emotional, pictorial, noble, universal and tonal, rising to the height of heaven and of feeling in the style traditionally known as grand or sublime.[32]

Whitman's common style is a secular variant of the sublime poem, God having been reduced to man, man then having been given some of the qualities once ascribed to God. Instead of aspiring to "the height of heaven," Whitman invokes earth and time and keeps on chanting. His fifty-odd most used words, by Josephine Miles's count, are: arm, beautiful, body, city, come, day, death, earth, eye, face, full, go, good, great, hand, hear, joy, know, land, life, light, long, look, love, make, man, night, old, pass, poem, real, rest, rise, sail, sea, see, ship, sing, soul, stand, strong, sun, take, thing, think, time, voice, war, woman, word, work, world, year, young. No sign of Spenser's *lady,* Milton's *angel,* Dryden's *heaven,* Wordsworth's *spirit.*

The unit in *Leaves of Grass* is the phrase, linked by a copula to the next one, and all kept moving by a verb, often repeated, often perfunctory, as in this passage from "Give Me the Splendid Silent Sun":

Keep your splendid silent sun,
Keep your woods O nature, and the quiet places by the woods,
Keep your fields of clover and timothy, and your corn-fields and orchards,
Keep the blossoming buckwheat fields where the Ninth-month bees hum;
Give me faces and streets—give me these phantoms incessant and endless along the trottoirs!
Give me interminable eyes—give me women—give me comrades and lovers by the thousand!
Let me see new ones every day—let me hold new ones by the hand every day!

Give me such shows—give me the streets of
 Manhattan![33]

Keep, Give, and *Let me see* are doing mundane work, setting the phrases going and holding the objects of the verbs more or less in place. The cognitive difference between keeping the sun (a decision no one is in a position to make) and keeping the woods (a feasible and decent thing to do) is lost. Only a niggardly reader would haggle over the point. We are meant to submit to the imperative rhythm without stopping to ask what the imperatives are doing and what we are supposed to do in reply. When we read line 43 of "Crossing Brooklyn Ferry"—"The flags of all nations, the falling of them at sunset"—we have a choice. We can take the line as it comes without expecting it to have much to do with the lines before and after. Or we can complete the sentence by reaching back five lines to the verb, *Saw,* and sixteen lines back to the subject *I,* words we have probably forgotten, displaced as they have been by the greater interest of the intervening phrases. If we take the line as it comes, we appreciate its internal qualities: a line of fourteen syllables, divided six and eight; two plural nouns in the first part, answered by two singular nouns—including a verbal noun—in the second; the internal rhyme of *all* and *fall,* modulating the two parts; the fatality of cadence, phrase linked to phrase. *Saw* is doing journeyman work. If we compare Whitman's *keep* and *give,* in "Give Me the Splendid Silent Sun," with what Hopkins does for these verbs in "The Leaden Echo and the Golden Echo"—

How to kéep—is there ány any, is there none such, nowhere
known some, bow or brooch or braid or brace, láce,
latch or catch or key to keep
Back beauty, keep it, beauty, beauty, beauty, . . . from vanishing away? . . .
Give beauty back, beauty, beauty, beauty, back to God,
beauty's self and beauty's giver.[34]

—we see that Whitman is taking these verbs for granted while Hopkins is working them up, as in the stretch between *Give* and *giver,* to the pitch of achieved significance and force. Whitman's rhapsody blurs distinctions where they might be made. We think such distinctions valuable if we believe with Hopkins—or imagine our believing—that the glory of God is fulfilled in His having created a world of different things, each thing its extraordinary self. We don't think them especially valuable if we cherish with Whitman the rhapsodic intuition of their generality.

4

The poem that everybody reads in *Leaves of Grass* is "Song of Myself." When it first appeared in July 1855 it had no title and was not divided into sections. Passages were as short as one line, as long as sixty-eight lines, and of diverse lengths in between. Reading it in that edition, you think you are reading poetry, not a poem. In the 1867 edition it was divided into fifty-two sections.

Whitman gave it its present title in the 1881 edition. The title is misleading. The poem is not autobiographical; nor is it a memoir. The only fact one could deduce from it about the author is that he liked opera. Everything else has its origin in newspapers, prints, and books—the victory of the *Bonhomme Richard* under the command of John Paul Jones, the massacre of Texan soldiers at Alamo on March 27, 1836. Or it is imagined in generic narrative form—the runaway slave, the marriage of the trapper and the red girl, the twenty-eight young men bathing, the Negro driving a team of horses. Many of the remaining passages are fantasies of male homosexual experiences. The only force that binds the 1,336 lines together is the fact that Whitman thought of these things or imagined them to the degree of making them seem indistinguishable from himself.

There are many good reasons for loving "Song of Myself," especially if you want to be released from logic, judgment, weighing and measuring:

> Showing the best and dividing it from the worst age
>   vexes age,
> Knowing the perfect fitness and equanimity of things,
>   while they discuss I am silent, and go bathe and
>   admire myself.

Or if you like to be assured that there is in each of us a secret "Me myself" that does not disappear into its conditions:

Apart from the pulling and hauling stands what I am,
Stands amused, complacent, compassionating, idle,
  unitary,
Looks down, is erect, or bends an arm on an impalpable
  certain rest,
Looking with sidecurved head curious what will come
  next,
Both in and out of the game and watching and
  wondering at it.

The colloquial style guarantees that the "Me myself" need not be thought of as portentous or divined with a long face:

Loafe with me on the grass, loose the stop from your
  throat,
Not words, not music or rhyme I want, not custom or
  lecture, not even the best,
Only the lull I like, the hum of your valvèd voice.[35]

These lines, addressed to "my soul," invoke a song-without-words, a communication as if prior to speech and the Fall into words. It is love at the first discovery of itself, the letter *l* is a promise of other letters, syllables, and words, but for the moment it delights in itself: leaves of grass, loafe, loose,—but not lecture—*lull* murmuring to the rhyme of *hum* and the assonance of *valvèd.* But mostly, it appears, readers of "Song of Myself" love to be told, even if they can't believe it, that evil is merely (as Emerson says in "Fate") good in the making.

"Song of Myself" is not, as it has been said to be, an epic, or even an epitome of an epic. It is a lyric suite, giving such credence to its moods and transitions that it might be performed as a tone poem. Its enabling device is not—not quite—the listing of entities. It is the litany. If Whitman were a Roman Catholic he would be heard praying to the Blessed Virgin in the litany dedicated to her—

Tower of Ivory,
House of Gold,
Ark of the Covenant,
Gate of Heaven,
Morning Star

—a prayer in which the motives of piety and supplication would not be thwarted if the invocations came in a different order, Gate of Heaven opening before the House of Gold. Whitman made up his own litanies, songs of the earth:

Smile O voluptuous cool-breathed earth!
Earth of the slumbering and liquid trees!
Earth of departed sunset—earth of the mountains
  misty-topt!
Earth of the vitreous pour of the full moon just tinged
  with blue!
Earth of shine and dark mottling the tide of the river!

Earth of the limpid gray of clouds brighter and clearer
for my sake!
Far-swooping elbow'd earth—Rich, apple-blossomed
earth!
Smile, for your lover comes![36]

This poetry does not describe qualities of the earth already there: it posits qualities so far as they are answerable to Whitman's desire and exempt from anyone's judgment. Claiming that his desire is representative—of desire as such and in general—he claims to have promulgated a new and better world than the one ordained by syntax and predication. Serial invocations repeal the laws of difference.

But my choice reason of the several reasons for loving this poem is the quiet audacity of its ending:

Listener up there! what have you to confide
to me?
Look in my face while I snuff the sidle of evening,
(Talk honestly, for no one else hears you, and I stay
only a minute longer.)

Do I contradict myself?
Very well then I contradict myself,
(I am large, I contain multitudes.)

I concentrate toward them that are nigh, I wait on the
door-slab.

Who has done his day's work? who will soonest be
through with his supper?
Who wishes to walk with me?

Will you speak before I am gone? will you prove already
too late?

The spotted hawk swoops by and accuses me, he
complains of my gab and my loitering.

I too am not a bit tamed, I too am untranslatable,
I sound my barbaric yawp over the roofs of the world.

The last scud of day holds back for me,
It flings my likeness after the rest and true as any on the
shadow'd wilds,
It coaxes me to the vapor and the dusk.

I depart as air, I shake my white locks at the runaway
sun,
I effuse my flesh in eddies, and drift it in lacy jags.

I bequeath myself to the dirt to grow from the grass
I love,
If you want me again look for me under your
boot-soles.

You will hardly know who I am or what I mean,
But I shall be good health to you nevertheless,
And filter and fibre your blood.

Failing to fetch me at first keep encouraged,
Missing me one place search another,
I stop somewhere waiting for you

No full stop brings this to an end in the first edition. The ending of *Finnegans Wake* is the only passage I can think of comparing, where again the elements of which it is composed drift off with Anna Livia to Dublin Bay, as to Whitman's indefinitely suspended "waiting . . . " As in most of Whitman's poetry, we are gathered up into the poet's voice, so that we hardly ask what it is saying. No particular situation is implied, the "you" is as abstract, as stylized, as the "I." But certain details are—unusually for Whitman—realized with extraordinary delicacy. "Look in my face while I snuff the sidle of evening." Sidle: as the evening may be thought to sidle—to move quietly, surreptitiously, toward the night. Snuff: as a baby or a young animal leans in upon the source of warmth. And then, with a different kind of authority, the spotted hawk swoops by: not down but by.

5

The political bearing of *Leaves of Grass* is not its documentation of a democratic society already in place and proving its worth without argument. After the Civil War, the assassination of Lincoln, and the approach of the Gilded Age, Whitman could locate democracy only in a future to be summoned to come forth, a world without obstacles, universally transparent. It is his version of the imaginary. In the preface of 1876 to *Leaves of Grass and Two Rivulets* he wrote:

> I count with such absolute certainty on the Great Future of The United States—different from, though founded on, the past—that I have always invoked that Future, and surrounded myself with it, before or while singing my Songs . . . . (As ever, all tends to followings—America, too, is a prophecy. What, even of the best and most successful, would be justified by itself alone? by the present, or the material ostent alone? Of men or States, few realize how much they live in the future. That, rising like pinnacles, gives its main significance to all You and I are doing to-day . . . . All ages, all Nations and States, have been such prophecies. But where any former ones with prophecy so broad, so clear, as our times, our lands—as those of the West?)[37]

That is not how he sounded in the preface of 1855: "The United States themselves are essentially the greatest poem," he claimed, singing an old song of Emerson's: "America is a poem in our eyes." If it is, it is a poem long since disfigured by stanzas featuring murderous adventures in the Philippines, Chile, El Salvador, Guatemala, Nicaragua, Vietnam, Afghanistan, Iraq (to name a few, with probably more to come). In the preface of 1876 Whitman is whistling, wheezing in the dark to ward off the ghosts. He knows the cost of his Utopia, his fantasy of the end of history, politics, and ideology; his vision of male bonding as the archetype of "these States." The future he calls forth is a future that need not happen. Its main value to him is to keep him going while he mistakes hope for truth.

In 1963 Louis Simpson published a collection of his poems, *At the End of the Open Road.* One of the poems was "Walt Whitman at Bear Mountain," in which Simpson—or someone—speaks to the "poet of death and lilacs" and tells him that "The Open Road goes to the used-car lot." "Where is the nation you promised?" The old poet remonstrates:

> "I gave no prescriptions,
> And those who have taken my moods for prophecies
> Mistake the matter."

But Simpson refuses to take the moods lightly:

> Then all the realtors,
> Pickpockets, salesmen, and the actors performing
> Official scenarios,
> Turned a deaf ear, for they had contracted
> American dreams.

Whitman has nothing more to say in this conversation, and Simpson is left to make the best of a bad American century:

> All that grave weight of America
> Cancelled! Like Greece and Rome.
> The future in ruins!
> The castles, the prisons, the cathedrals
> Unbuilding, and roses
> Blossoming from the stones that are not there . . .

At the end, Simpson turns his eyes from the used-car lot, the doomed prophecies, the wretched American dreams:

> The clouds are lifting from the high Sierras,
> The Bay mists clearing.
> And the angel in the gate, the flowering plum,
> Dances like Italy, imagining red.[38]

Simpson is trying to get rid of a bad mood, lest it settle into a bad prophecy. The angel is not dancing but weeping.

Why? I think the reason is well expressed in two passages, a few pages apart, in William H. Gass's essay on Emerson. In the first, Gass notes that Emerson was preoccupied with the problem of the Fall:

> In this new clime—America—with Calvin presumably put back aboard ship and sent home to the Swiss, what one was most free from was sin; one could not blame

> Eve again, or any ancient crime; yet that meant that the responsibility for failure fell on us like an enemy from ambush; and if death was with us despite our sinless state, in the stalk and leaf, the blood, the flesh, real as the last rattle of the breath, then the general injustice was that for an imaginary malfeasance in a legendary age, we were to be hung tomorrow from a loop of quite unimaginary rope.[39]

The second passage calls for a little commentary. It starts from a phrase of Emerson's:

> "The universal impulse to believe," as Emerson both manifested and expressed it, was as positive in his time as it is negative in ours, because beliefs are our pestilence. Skepticism, these days, is the only intelligence. The vow of a fool—never to be led astray or again made a fool of—is our commonest resolution. Doubt, disbelief, detachment, irony, scorn, measure our disappointment, since mankind has proved even a poorer god than those which did not exist.[40]

That is worth saying, if not imperatively worth believing. It is particularly germane to a reading of Whitman and Emerson. Readers of "Song of Myself" are neither better nor worse fools than other people, but what they enjoy in the poem is the experience of imagining what it would be to believe something that seems worth believing. What Whitman believed as an editor, a propagandist, a post-Emersonian chauvinist is not, in my view, worth believing. It is mostly a pestilence. But the experience of "going along" with him, notionally and provisionally, in reaching that belief and voicing it is eminently worth having. Fortunately, I am not obliged to join his army.

6

Adventures of Huckleberry Finn

I

I've mentioned that with *American Renaissance* (1941) Matthiessen established that America had a literature: specifically, that in the middle of the nineteenth century America for the first time produced a literature—and therefore a culture—to be acknowledged as such. Not that the country had lacked good writers till 1855; but they had not come together in their differences to make a declaration of literary and cultural independence. Emerson, Hawthorne, Melville, and Whitman made a literature, such that earlier and later American writers might be construed in relation to one or another of those four, as Henry James might be read in relation to Hawthorne, and Whitman and Thoreau in relation to Emerson. But Matthiessen did not claim that the books written by these writers amounted to a comprehensive literature or that the culture they embodied was complete. It soon became common for scholars of American literature to speak of "the disunity of the American creative mind" and to offer terms for understanding that condition. "Viewed historically," Philip Rahv said, "American writers appear to group themselves around polar types." He called them paleface and redskin, and started with the contrast between James and Whitman, as between Melville and Mark Twain. "At one pole," Rahv noted, "there is the literature of the lowlife world of the frontier and of the big cities; at the other the thin, solemn, semi-clerical culture of Boston and Concord." The process of polarization was evidence of "a dichotomy between experience and consciousness—a dissociation between energy and sensibility, between conduct and theories of conduct, between life conceived as an opportunity and life conceived as a discipline":

> The paleface continually hankers after religious norms, tending toward a refined estrangement from reality. The redskin accepts his environment, at times to the degree of fusion with it, even when rebelling against one or another of its manifestations. At his highest level the paleface moves in an exquisite moral atmosphere; at his lowest he is genteel, snobbish, and pedantic. In giving expression to the vitality and to the aspirations of the people, the redskin is at his best; but at his worst he is a vulgar anti-intellectual, combining aggression with conformity and reverting to the crudest forms of frontier psychology.[1]

Sociologically, the difference is between patricians and plebeians; rhetorically, it is a difference between writers who resort to symbolism and allegory and writers who incline to "a gross, riotous naturalism." Rahv's palefaces are Hawthorne, Melville, Emily Dickinson, Henry James, and T. S. Eliot. His redskins are Whitman, Mark Twain, Dreiser, Sherwood Anderson, Sinclair Lewis, Thomas Wolfe, Erskine Caldwell, and Steinbeck. Rahv wondered whether or not history would make whole again what it had rent asunder. A complete human image required such unity. Meanwhile the fracture of American culture had to be understood. Rahv did not dispute Matthiessen's findings or the canon of American literature he proposed. It was a matter for other scholars to suggest additions or amendments to it, and to ponder the fragmenting of culture that persisted through particular acts of apprehension. The canon did not guarantee that the culture it embodied was coherent.

Among the possible additions to the canon there was the question of Cooper, about whom Matthiessen had little to say. If you were persuaded by D. H. Lawrence's *Studies in Classic American Literature,* Cooper could not be omitted. Conrad praised him as a rare artist, a great storyteller. Yvor Winters took him seriously for even more reasons than those. Marius Bewley and Donald Davie argued that Cooper was an artist on the same level of achievement as Scott, Hawthorne, Melville, and James. I can only report my own experience of reading Cooper. My determination to respect the cultural significance of Natty Bumppo and Chingachgook barely enabled me to keep turning the pages of *The Pioneers, The Last of the Mohicans, The Prairie, The Pathfinder,* and *The Deerslayer.* I found those books nearly unreadable, even in a mood of righteousness and duty. Mark Twain's "Fenimore Cooper's Literary Offenses" seemed to me not a mere squib but an irrefutable essay in criticism. I felt relief when I was assured, at the beginning of *The Prairie,* that I was about to come to the end of the Leatherstocking tales. It was also a blessing to find Leslie Fiedler saying, in *Love and Death in the American Novel,* that "Cooper had, alas, all the qualifications for a great American writer except the simple ability to write."[2] Not that Mark Twain and Fiedler were the only critics to tell the truth about Cooper's style. Poe said of Cooper's *Wyandotte; or, The Hutted Knoll* that its most obvious faults "are those which appertain to the *style,* to the mere grammatical construction. . . . His sentences are arranged with an awkwardness so remarkable as to be matter of absolute astonishment, when we consider the education of the author, and his long and continual practice with the pen."[3] The prestige of Cooper as a major novelist is to be explained not by his literary power but by the need of American readers to feel that they have made their peace with the native Americans. As a novelist, Cooper seems to me not at all as good as Patrick O'Brian.

There was also the question of Mark Twain, another writer only occasionally mentioned in Matthiessen's book. He is usually considered the supreme exemplar of Midwest humor, but that claim is a minor one; it cannot exert much force in a comparison with Emerson, Thoreau, Hawthorne, Melville, and Whitman. Or he is praised for having brought the resources of casual, substandard, or "vernacular" speech to bear upon the complacency of the "genteel tradition." That is a more formidable issue. But again it is equivocal. The genteel tradition has not been disabled. But in 1952 and again in 1955 F. R. Leavis made a far higher claim for Twain than one could have anticipated. So far as I know, the claim has not been much debated. Leavis's occasion in 1955 was his writing an introduction to *Pudd'nhead Wilson*. In 1952 it was the publication of Marius Bewley's *The Complex Fate*, for which Leavis provided an introduction, a disagreement, and a further comment. In that book Bewley maintained that the "school of literary appreciation which acclaims American literature simply because it is American has been represented by a strong body of critical opinion in the United States, and it has led to an insidious magnification of the frontier colloquial tradition in American literature." That tradition, Bewley conceded, is one of some force, but "it is not the tradition embodied in America's four major novelists"—he meant Cooper, Hawthorne, Melville, and James:

> This frontier tradition has its own high points of achievement, but it represents the extreme isolationism of American literature, and it is fragmentary and misleading because it does not provide sufficient scope in itself to treat the largest problem that confronted the American artist in the nineteenth century, and which

still occupies him: the nature of his separateness, and the nature of his connection with European, and particularly with English, culture.[4]

Bewley was mainly concerned with Hawthorne and James, and he reserved for a later book, *The Eccentric Design: Form in the Classic American Novel,* what he had to say about Cooper and Melville. But Leavis, introducing *The Complex Fate,* pushed Bewley toward a degree of explicitness perhaps higher than he had bargained for when he invited Leavis to intervene on specific issues—local disagreements on *What Maisie Knew* and, briefly, "The Turn of the Screw." Leavis argued that when the "frontier tradition" is made the source of a "truly American literature," the idea derives "an illicit respectability from the aura of Mark Twain." When it is exalted in that way, "what we have (it is enough to note) is the spirit of which it may be said that its essential definition of Americanness is given in the collocation of Whitman, Dreiser, Scott Fitzgerald and Hemingway." Leavis dismissed those writers, and separated Mark Twain from them, insisting that the fellowship to which Twain truly belongs is that of Bewley's four, Cooper, Hawthorne, Melville, and James. When *The Eccentric Design* appeared in 1959, it became clear that Bewley had a higher appreciation of Fitzgerald than Leavis had, but the issue between them on that score was not joined. In his introduction to *The Complex Fate* Leavis asserted that in Fitzgerald's world "no vestige, and no suspicion, of any standard of maturity exists." But he remarked, just as strongly, "the portentous distance between Hemingway and Mark Twain." The author of *Huckleberry Finn* "writes out of a full cultural heritage." Compared with the idiom cultivated by Hemingway, "Huck's language, as he speaks it, it is hardly excessive to say, is Shakespearean in its range and subtlety":

> Mark Twain, of course, has made of the colloquial mode he took such pride in rendering accurately a convention of art and a literary medium. But in doing so he has achieved an inevitable naturalness; the achievement, in fact, is the creation of Huck himself, about whom, I imagine, it has rarely been complained that he is unconvincing. And in Huck, the embodiment of an ungenteel western vernacular, he has made a *persona* for the expression of a mature criticism of life—-mature and subtle by the standards of the great European literatures.[5]

It follows from those last phrases—in which the moral emphases of Matthew Arnold and T. S. Eliot are evident—that Twain, as the author of *Huckleberry Finn* and *Pudd'nhead Wilson,* is brought into the tradition of Cooper, Hawthorne, Melville, and James and made to appear equal to them in moral and critical significance.

Bewley did not publish an essay on Twain, because "what there is to say positively of his achievement has been registered by T. S. Eliot, F. R. Leavis, and Lionel Trilling in their respective introductions and essays," and because "he is not a writer who comes to terms easily with literary analysis."[6] This latter is a strange reason for silence and may be thought to reflect either on Twain or on the poverty of literary analysis, especially as the merit that Leavis, Eliot, and Trilling emphasized in Twain was his invention of a new way of writing. Eliot went farthest in this direction: "Twain, at least in *Huckleberry Finn,* reveals himself to be one of those writers, of whom there are not a great many in any literature, who have discovered a new way of writing, valid not only for themselves but for others." The consideration in that last phrase invited comparison of Twain, Eliot said, with Dryden and Swift as "one of those rare writers who have brought their language up to date, and in so doing, 'purified the dialect of the tribe.'" The corresponding contrast was with Whitman and Hopkins, writers who found an idiom and a metric "perfectly suited for what they had to say" but "very doubtfully adaptable to what anyone else has to say."[7]

The values embodied in Bewley's four major writers included not merely the characteristic American experience they confronted but the spirit in which they dealt with it:

> "The new American experience" that Cooper, Hawthorne, Melville, and James had dealt with had been, above all else, an inward thing: and it was inward, not with the professional curiosity of the Freudian, who came later, nor the impertinent inquisitiveness of the sociologist, but with the deeply humane recognition that the problems that tormented them as American artists

> had first to be confronted in the solitude of their own souls. They were all great moralists, great critics in their art, and, in their own way, metaphysicians; and the reality they sought to explore was where the sociological novelists, the naturalists and the documentarians, could never follow them.[8]

It is not surprising, with this emphasis before us, that the American poet whom Bewley found especially to have cared for the "inward thing" in relation to the forces that threatened it was Wallace Stevens, and that the commitment of that care was a commitment to the postromantic or Coleridgean imagination. As Bewley put it in *The Complex Fate:*

> It is in relation to his sense of the catastrophic fragmentariness of the contemporary world that [Stevens's] belief in the unifying power of the imagination has achieved such rare distinction. It cannot, in the nature of the case, offer a solution theoretically as complete as Eliot's Christianity, but it does offer a reality that sometimes seems to be almost the unbaptized blood-brother of Eliot's reality—and it is a reality that finds frequent, but by no means invariable, realization in the poetry itself.[9]

It will hardly be thought probable that Mark Twain's terms of reference and invocation coincide with Stevens's or with Bewley's. Twain's work has metaphysical implications, but he was not a metaphysician in the resolute sense we associate with Stevens as the author of *The Necessary Angel* and "Notes Toward a Supreme Fiction." But if we are to take Leavis and Bewley at their words, where Twain is in question, we see him attending, as Stevens did more formally, to the relation between imagination and reality, and to the prior enabling and unifying power he ascribed to the imagination. Without such a commitment, Twain could hardly be thought of in relation to the "inward thing" that Bewley finds so compelling in his four major novelists. But while the "inward thing" is clear in Stevens under the name of imagination, it is harder to specify in Twain. It seems to me that it is what he called, in one of his notebooks, not a creative capacity but "a sound heart," and that reality as the opposing term is the concatenation of social forces that issued in what he called "a deformed conscience."

In 1895, nearly twenty years after he began work on *Huckleberry Finn,* Twain described it as "a book of mine where a sound heart & a deformed conscience come into collision & conscience suffers defeat." The defeat of such a conscience—if we can call it a conscience—is to be welcomed. "The conscience—that unerring monitor—can be trained to approve any wild thing you *want* it to approve if you begin its education early & stick to it."[10] In another note Twain wrote of the conscience: "It is merely a *thing;* the creature of *training;* it is whatever one's mother and Bible and comrades and laws and system of government and habitat and heredities have made it. It is not a separate person, it has no originality, no independence."[11] The deformed conscience keeps going by imitating what it finds in newspapers, gossip, and the common lore; and by projecting the fantasies that accompany those sources. The crudest thing a deformed conscience was ready to approve, in the characters in *Tom Sawyer* and *Huckleberry Finn* and the society they constituted, was slavery. "In those old slave-holding days the whole community"—Twain meant the white people—"was agreed as to one thing—the awful sacredness of slave property":

> To help steal a horse or a cow was a low crime, but to help a hunted slave, or feed him or shelter him, or hide him or comfort him, in his troubles, his terrors, his despair, or hesitate to promptly betray him to the slave-catcher when opportunity offered was a much baser crime, & carried with it a stain, a moral smirch which nothing could wipe away.[12]

The conscience that approved slavery, took it for granted and practiced it, was gradually defeated, first by the Civil War, then by a national and international zeitgeist that found the system of slavery morally repellent, and later (however haltingly) by the Supreme Court and legislation under the presidencies of (mainly) Truman, Eisenhower, Kennedy, and Johnson. But the racist prejudice that made the war and the legislation necessary has not ceased, it has merely become a consideration of class distinctions, in which middle-class and upper-class people of whatever color are socially acceptable, but people of lower class are not. In the short run, Huck defeated the deformed conscience or at least rejected it in himself for friendship's sake, but he succumbed to one of its forms—which he found in Tom Sawyer—for most of the book. Informally, a sound heart is common decency, but that, too, has to be explained. Or else it is an innate capacity, differing not in kind but in degree between one person and another as a commonplace mind differs from genius. Twain explained how a conscience became deformed, but not how one acquired a sound heart under the same conditions.

In *Tom Sawyer, Huckleberry Finn,* and *Pudd'nhead Wilson,* to confine ourselves to the novels for which such a claim as Leavis's has been made, the deformed conscience enforces itself as the moral and social norm. It is enthralled by the theater of appearances, as the duel between Judge Driscoll and Luigi Capello in *Pudd'nhead Wilson* makes clear. When Roxana, in that novel, switches the infants Thomas and Chambers—one white, the other black—in their cradles, she starts a process by which the spurious "Thomas," as he grows up, is accepted in Dawson's Landing for what he is not, and treated as if he were the true son of Percy Driscoll and his wife. In the end, the lawyer David Wilson exposes him for what he is, with the aid of the new science of fingerprinting. "Thomas" confesses to the murder of Judge Driscoll, and is pardoned only to be sold down the river. Chambers, the true heir, comes into his own, but—Twain will have nothing to do with a fairy-tale ending—he can't enjoy his riches, and the last we hear of him is that he is lost in all the scenes available to him:

> The real heir suddenly found himself rich and free, but in a most embarrassing situation. He could neither read nor write, and his speech was the basest dialect of the Negro quarter. His gait, his attitudes, his gestures, his bearing, his laugh—all were vulgar and uncouth; his manners were the manners of a slave. Money and fine clothes could not mend these defects or cover them up, they only made them the more glaring and the more pathetic. The poor fellow could not endure the terrors of the white man's parlour, and felt at home and at peace nowhere but in the kitchen. The family pew was a misery to him, yet he could nevermore enter into the solacing refuge of the "nigger gallery"—that was closed to him for good and all.[13]

The deformed conscience is continuously active in Tom Sawyer, who is a conformist despite his mischief and roguery. He is thoroughly at home in the society he seems to irritate. Tom is as susceptible to the melodramatic literature of derring-do and piracy he reads as Emma Bovary is to the romances of the day, but he is a mere gamester. He is not a threat to the social practices of Aunt Polly, Mr. Walters, the Widow Douglas, and Judge Thatcher. Aunt Sally and Uncle Silas are decent, neighborly people, but they feel no scruple about keeping the runaway slave Jim locked up in the hut by the ash hopper, fed on bread and water and loaded down with chains till he's claimed or sold. At the end of the book Tom imposes his social amenity on Huck: "But, Huck, we can't let you into the gang if you ain't respectable, you know." When Huck protests and asks Tom not to shut him out, Tom says: "Huck, I wouldn't want to and I don't want to, but what would people say? Why, they'd say, 'Mph! Tom Sawyer's Gang! Pretty low characters in it!' They'd mean you, Huck. You wouldn't like that, and I wouldn't." Huck is so intimidated by Tom that he promises to go back to the Widow for at least a month and see if he can stand it, "if you'll let me b'long to the gang, Tom."[14] In *Adventures of Huckleberry Finn* when Huck meets Tom again, in chapter 33, Tom takes over the show and devises more and more elaborate contrivances to keep Jim locked up and to postpone his release. Many readers have been appalled by the part of the novel in which Tom and Huck engage in these tricks at Jim's expense. They think that these chapters turn into farce "the most serious motive in the novel, Jim's yearning for freedom."[15] Or they think, as Richard Poirier does, that after chapter 16 the book goes to pieces because Huck's voice becomes increasingly inaudible and the novel is no longer the autobiography of Huck Finn: "It must instead become a kind of documentation of why the consciousness of the hero cannot be developed in dramatic relations to any element of this society":

> What Mark Twain discovered at the point of his famous and prolonged difficulties after Chapter XV was that even his limited effort to create an environment alterna-

> tive to the shore had made his task impossible. He must, finally, "insert" Huck back into his customary environment. He must, in effect, destroy him. Huck as a character, created mostly in his soliloquies up through Chapter XV, is replaced by another figure, using the same name, but able to exist within the verbal world of the last two thirds of the novel, a world demonstrably less free than the verbal world or environment of the first third.[16]

But the question that Poirier raises without answering is: why could Twain not find a voice for the disenchanted phase of Huck's experience? The contrast between *Huckleberry Finn* and *Emma*, as Poirier describes it, is that Jane Austen found in the social world the values that enabled Emma to detect herself. Emma falls in with the theatricality of Frank Churchill and commits the self-regarding cruelty of her insult to Miss Bates. But under the guidance of Knightley, she convicts herself in the social terms in which she has erred. Mark Twain, apparently, could not imagine such terms, because they had already been appropriated by Tom Sawyer. This can only mean that the culture inhabited by Jane Austen was comprehensive—and therefore morally enabling—in a sense in which Mark Twain's, despite Leavis's praise of it, was not. Poirier argues that the stress on language, in the major American novels and poems, is explained by that predicament. It is only in language, not in the culture which sustains language, that freedom and the consciousness of freedom are to be achieved. Hence the disjunction between experience and consciousness to which Rahv refers. But this does not explain why Twain, unlike Melville and Whitman, was unable to imagine such freedom for his hero even in a language that supposedly floats free of the environment that otherwise disfigures it.

Fiedler has endorsed the end of the book on the grounds that "the essential virtue of Huck and Jim is to endure whatever befalls them; and to them, moreover, there is nothing any more ridiculous about what Tom does than there is about what society inflicts on them every day."[17] But Huck and Jim don't see what Tom does as ridiculous; they can't separate themselves from the shenanigans to that extent. A better defense of these chapters is needed. Twain is showing, I think, how dogged the deformed conscience is and how persistent it is in what it does not even recognize as cruelty. The chapters are not tedious if we read them as evidence of how nearly this conscience comes to winning, in a society typified at its best by the Phelpses.

Huck is tainted by the deformed conscience throughout the book, though not as continuously as Tom, who exemplifies it. The deformed conscience accounts for Huck's practical jokes on Jim, and shadows his apologies for having played them. When Huck is cruel to Jim, it is because he is imitating Tom Sawyer. His desire to hurt Jim is not spontaneous, it is—as René Girard would say—mimetic, it is his desire to be Tom, to speak his language, to adopt his style. In chapter 16 his conscience starts up again and he thinks of turning Jim in:

> Jim said it made him all over trembly and feverish to be so close to freedom. Well, I can tell you it made me all over trembly and feverish, too, to hear him, because I begun to get it through my head that he *was* most free—and who was to blame for it? Why, *me*. I couldn't get that out of my conscience, no how nor no way. It got to troubling me so I couldn't rest; I couldn't stay still in one place. It hadn't ever come home to me before, what this thing was that I was doing. But now it did; and it staid with me, and scorched me more and more. I tried to make out to myself that *I* warn't to blame, because *I* didn't run Jim off from his rightful owner, but it warn't no use, conscience up and says, every time, "But you knowed he was running for his freedom, and you could a paddled ashore and told somebody."[18]

When Jim is caught and locked up in Silas Phelps's place and Huck hears of it, he thinks of sending word to Miss Watson to tell her where Jim is:

> But I soon give up that notion, for two things: she'd be mad and disgusted at his rascality and ungratefulness for leaving her, and so she'd sell him straight down the river again; and if she didn't, everybody naturally despises an ungrateful nigger, and they'd make Jim feel it all the time, and so he'd feel ornery and disgraced. And then think of *me!* It would get all around, that Huck Finn

> helped a nigger to get his freedom; and if I was to ever see anybody from that town again, I'd be ready to get down and lick his boots for shame. That's just the way: a person does a low-down thing, and then he don't want to take no consequences of it. Thinks as long as he can hide it, it ain't no disgrace. That was my fix exactly. The more I studied about this, the more my conscience went to grinding me, and the more wicked, and low-down and ornery I got to feeling. And at last, when it hit me all of a sudden that here was the plain hand of Providence slapping me in the face and letting me know my wickedness was being watched all the time from up there in heaven, whilst I was stealing a poor old woman's nigger that hadn't ever done me no harm, and now was showing me there's One that's always on the lookout, and ain't agoing to allow no such miserable doings to go only just so fur and no further, I most dropped in my tracks I was so scared.

The irony of this turns on the sense we have had of Huck up to this point—of his independence and "sound heart"—and now of his capitulation to a conscience socially defined and corrupt. His yielding to the opinion of "everybody," his considering that his action "would get around," his respect for Miss Watson's property—"a poor old woman's nigger"—reduces for the time being the moral difference between Huck and Tom. Huck writes the letter to Miss Watson—"Miss Watson your runaway nigger Jim is down here two mile below Pikesville and Mr. Phelps has got him and he will give him up for the reward if you send. HUCK FINN." The immediate effect on Huck of his writing the letter is a conviction of being saved: "I felt good and all washed clean of sin for the first time I had ever felt so in my life, and I knowed I could pray, now. But I didn't do it straight off, but laid the paper down and set there thinking; thinking how good it was all this happened so, and how near I come to being lost and going to hell." But then Huck starts recalling the happy scenes with Jim on the raft, Jim's "standing my watch on top of his'n," Jim's pleasure when Huck came back out of the fog, "and how good he always was":

> And at last I struck the time I saved him by telling the men we had small-pox aboard, and he was so grateful, and said I was the best friend old Jim ever had in the world, and the *only* one he's got now; and then I happened to look around, and see that paper.

"All right, then, I'll *go* to hell," and he tears up the letter. The sound heart has won out over the deformed conscience, at least for now. Huck knows that the friendship he has enjoyed with Jim has a far stronger claim on him than the social conventions by which he is supposed to live. It wins out again when, in response to Tom's plan of going "for howling adventures amongst the Injuns, over in the Territory, for a couple of weeks or two," Huck decides to "light out for the Territory ahead of the rest," ahead of Tom and with no time limit set.[19]

2

The aim common to Leavis and Bewley was to rescue Twain from the company of naturalists—Rahv's redskins—to which literary historians regularly consigned him. Eliot's commentaries on Twain anticipated that aim, though they did not address it directly. Eliot was not concerned to see Twain keep better company, but the effect of the way in which he read *Tom Sawyer, Huckleberry Finn,* and *Life on the Mississippi* was to move Twain closer to Joyce than to Dreiser. Eliot interpreted those books under the auspices of anthropology rather than of history, politics, or morality.

It is not clear when Eliot first read Twain. In his introduction to the Cresset Press printing of *Huckleberry Finn* (1950) he said that he did not read *Tom Sawyer* and *Huckleberry Finn* in his childhood but "only a few years ago." That suggests that he wrote "The Dry Salvages"—beginning in December 1940—without benefit of Twain and relying mainly on his memory of childhood years in St. Louis and boyhood vacations near Cape Ann. When he came to write about Twain, in 1950 and 1953, he went back to the themes and the vocabulary of "The Dry Salvages" and interpreted Twain's books in the light of that poem. It is likely that Trilling's introduction to *Huckleberry Finn,* published in 1948, helped to turn

Eliot in that direction. Eliot did not hold himself obliged to keep up to date on the scholarship of the topics he wrote about, but he was willing to read a few things if someone recommended them. When I had a meeting with him at the old office of Faber and Faber, 24 Russell Square, London, he asked me to suggest some books or essays he might find useful for the British Council booklet he had agreed to write on George Herbert. I sent him an essay by L. C. Knights and one by Kenneth Burke. When the booklet came out, it showed no sign that Eliot had found the essays worth thinking about. Maybe he didn't read them. But he may have read Trilling's essay on *Huckleberry Finn* and taken it seriously, and I think he did, if only because it was clearly inspired by "The Dry Salvages." Quoting that poem, Trilling anticipates Eliot in his meditation on the river, the river god, and the nature of gods.

The origin of Eliot's essay on *Huckleberry Finn* is evidently the first lines of "The Dry Salvages":

> I do not know much about gods; but I think that the river
> Is a strong brown god—sullen, untamed and intractable,
> Patient to some degree, at first recognised as a frontier;
> Useful, untrustworthy, as a conveyor of commerce;
> Then only a problem confronting the builder of
> bridges.[20]

In Eliot's essay, a comparison with Conrad keeps the tone of discursiveness going:

> Thus the River makes the book a great book. As with Conrad, we are continually reminded of the power and terror of Nature, and the isolation and feebleness of Man. Conrad remains always the European observer of the tropics, the white man's eye contemplating the Congo and its black gods. But Mark Twain is a native, and the River God is his God. It is as a native that he accepts the River God, and it is the subjection of Man that gives to Man his dignity. For without some kind of God, Man is not even very interesting.[21]

This is a strange outburst. It is remarkable to find Eliot, in 1950—late in his Christian years—giving such significance to "some kind of God," as if the particular kind made no difference. Something of the asperity of his essay on Baudelaire has intruded. It is as if Eliot were recalling his early years as a poet when the gods of anthropology—of *The Golden Bough* and *From Ritual to Romance*—were the only gods he thought of. This late meditation on Twain's river, the Mississippi, sent him back not only to the "strong brown god" of "The Dry Salvages" but to gods he had long since acknowledged if not prayed to. Not surprisingly, the moral of the meditation is "the subjection of man." In "The Dry Salvages" there is reference to "the river with its cargo of dead Negroes, cows and chicken coops." This can't be an allusion to the great scene in *Huckleberry Finn*—chapter 9—where Huck and Jim see a two-story derelict frame house floating down the river. They board the house by the second story and Jim finds a dead man shot in the back. He throws some old rags over him, because he recognizes him and wants to prevent Huck from seeing that it is his father, Pap. The reference in "The Dry Salvages" can't be an allusion; besides, the cargo is a white man, not a dead Negro. But both references come from the same region of experience, which Eliot invoked again in "American Literature and the American Language," referring to Twain's Mississippi as

> not only the river known to those who voyage on it or live beside it, but the universal river of human life—more universal, indeed, than the Congo of Joseph Conrad. . . . For Twain's readers anywhere, the Mississippi is *the* river. There is in Twain, I think, a great unconscious depth, which gives to *Huckleberry Finn* this symbolic value: a symbolism all the more powerful for being uncalculated and unconscious.[22]

The main difference between the meditation on the river in "The Dry Salvages" and in Eliot's essay is that in the poem the river leads to the sea, but in the essay it is not considered as doing so:

> The river is within us, the sea is all about us;
> The sea is the land's edge also, the granite
> Into which it reaches, the beaches where it tosses
> Its hints of earlier and other creation:
> The starfish, the horseshoe crab, the whale's backbone.[23]

In the essay, we hear little of the sea, even if it is all about us. We hear of the river, that with its strong, swift current it is the dictator to raft or steamboat:

> It is a treacherous and capricious dictator. At one season, it may move sluggishly in a channel so narrow that, encountering it for the first time at that point, one can hardly believe that it has traveled already for hundreds of miles, and has yet many hundreds of miles to go; at another season, it may obliterate the low Illinois shore to a horizon of water, while in its bed it runs with a speed such that no man or beast can survive in it. At such times, it carries down human bodies, cattle and houses.[24]

It carries Huck and Jim, too, down the river and will not let them land at Cairo, where Jim could have reached freedom.

I have described Eliot's reading of Twain as anthropological rather than moral, political, or social. To indicate what I mean, I'll quote part of Eliot's review of *Ulysses*, where he scolds Richard Aldington for getting the book wrong and draws Joyce away from the tradition of the realistic novel. Speaking of the myth, as Eliot calls it, the relation that Joyce maintains between the modern events of *Ulysses*—the events ascribed to June 16, 1904, in Dublin—and the main episodes in Homer's *Odyssey*, Eliot writes:

> In using the myth, in manipulating a continuous parallel between contemporaneity and antiquity, Mr. Joyce is

> pursuing a method which others must pursue after him. They will not be imitators, any more than the scientist who uses the discoveries of an Einstein in pursuing his own, independent, further investigations. It is simply a way of controlling, or ordering, of giving a shape and a significance to the immense panorama of futility and anarchy which is contemporary history. It is a method already adumbrated by Mr. Yeats, and of the need for which I believe Mr. Yeats to have been the first contemporary to be conscious. It is a method for which the horoscope is auspicious. Psychology (such as it is, and whether our reaction to it be comic or serious), ethnology, and *The Golden Bough* have concurred to make possible what was impossible even a few years ago. Instead of narrative method, we may now use the mythical method. It is, I seriously believe, a step toward making the modern world possible for art, toward that order and form which Mr. Aldington so earnestly desires.[25]

The method adumbrated by Mr. Yeats was, I think, that of such a poem as "No Second Troy," in which an unnamed modern woman—we may call her Maud Gonne—is juxtaposed in an unspecified relation to Helen of Troy. "Was there another Troy for her to burn?" The method is analogy, the putting of one thing beside another without a syntax that would make a relation between them specific. There is significance, but it is not designated.[26] It is the method of the double plot in Elizabethan drama, where two actions are brought together to make a third with some of the qualities of both. Eliot valued the method, it appears, because otherwise the thing focused upon is merely itself. It is the method he used when he put Tiresias in the position of foreseeing and foresuffering all in *The Waste Land:*

> (And I Tiresias have foresuffered all
> Enacted on this same divan or bed;
> I who have sat by Thebes below the wall
> And walked among the lowest of the dead.)[27]

Psychology, ethnology, and anthropology concurred to make this method possible because they permitted us to think of a thing not as impoverished by being merely what it is but as figuring in a pattern more comprehensive than itself. The penury of the thing is redeemed by the form, the pattern in which it plays a part. The sense of pattern in ourselves was one of Eliot's preoccupations, as in this passage on Marston's *Sophonisba:*

> In spite of the tumultuousness of the action, and the ferocity and horror of certain parts of the play, there is an underlying serenity; and as we familiarize ourselves with the play we perceive a pattern behind the pattern into which the characters deliberately involve themselves; the kind of pattern which we perceive in our

> own lives only at rare moments of inattention and detachment, drowsing in sunlight.[28]

That is where the gods come in, whether we call their intervention Fate or by some other name.

It is where the river flows, however capriciously, in *Huckleberry Finn.* It is also why Huck is, as Eliot calls him, "the spirit of the River."[29] He is not merely someone who goes down the Mississippi on a raft or a canoe or a steamboat and sometimes goes ashore for one reason or another. He partakes of the river in its divinity. What Eliot calls myth, in its bearing on *Ulysses,* is the story insofar as, starting by being merely a local story and without ceasing to be local, it becomes a story of life as such; it enacts and fulfills a pattern of life, universal and perennial. The mythical method, as Twain uses it, is a method by which *one* becomes *all* by analogical extension. The river makes this possible. In "The Dry Salvages" the sea adds to the mystery by abiding our question—why is there something rather than nothing?

This is obvious enough to anyone of a mythical, symbolic, or anthropological disposition. To anyone whose disposition is entirely social or political, it will appear obscurantist in not paying enough attention to characters and plots. Eliot paid attention to Huck and Jim, but only to the extent of seeing them in the anthropological perspective of the river god. "Huck Finn is alone: there is no more solitary character in fiction," Eliot says. But beyond that, Eliot tends to see the characters of fiction as emanations of the anthropological perspective that supervises them rather than as characters or personalities in their own social right. His account of *Ulysses* has nothing to say of Bloom, Stephen Dedalus, or Molly Bloom. The mythical method sets up an overarching authority, such that local events are construed under its sign. Huck is a certain kind of consciousness, because the mythical authority that Eliot invokes is a greater degree of the same kind of consciousness. It follows that "Huck is passive and impassive, apparently always the victim of events; and yet, in his acceptance of his world and of what it does to him and others, he is more powerful than his world, because he is more *aware* than any other person in it."[30] Huck is lonely because he is an isolated consciousness, isolation being a condition of his being conscious at all. A reader whose axioms are entirely social and political will have none of this. Leo Marx refuses to think of Twain's Mississippi as anything but a river, water in motion, a means of transport. Eliot's talk of the river and the river god seems to Marx "an extravagant view of the function of the neutral agency of the river":

> Clemens had a knowledgeable respect for the Mississippi and, without sanctifying it, was able to provide excellent reasons for Huck's and Jim's intense relation with it. It is a source of food and beauty and terror and serenity of mind. But, above all, it provides motion; it is the means by which Huck and Jim move away from a menacing civilization. They return to the river to continue their

> journey. The river cannot, does not, supply purpose. That purpose is a facet of their consciousness, and without the motive of escape from society, *Huckleberry Finn* would indeed "be only a sequence of adventures."[31]

But Eliot did not claim that the river supplies purpose: the energy of the river, as of the river god, is not lavished on our welfare, it is indifferent to our purpose. Leo Marx is one of the forgetful people reflected upon in the first section of "The Dry Salvages":

> The problem once solved, the brown god is almost
> forgotten
> By the dwellers in cities—ever, however, implacable,
> Keeping his seasons and rages, destroyer, reminder
> Of what men choose to forget. Unhonoured,
> unpropitiated
> By worshippers of the machine, but waiting, watching
> and waiting.[32]

If Marx thinks this is mere mystification, there is no possibility of resolving the dispute. To Eliot, Twain's river is not "neutral."

3

How, then, should one read *Huckleberry Finn?* "When we are considering poetry," Eliot said, "we must consider it primarily as poetry and not another thing. . . . [It] is not the inculcation of morals, or the direction of politics, and no more is it religion or an equivalent of religion, except by some monstrous abuse of words. . . . A poem, in some sense, has its own life."[33] The passage is qualified by "primarily" and "in some sense," but in its general bearing it holds out against the inclination to treat a poem or a work of fiction as merely an instrument in the furtherance of the politics, religion, or morals it appears to recommend. The particular merit of Eliot's reading of *Huckleberry Finn*—and of Leavis's, too—is that it respects the work as a poem, a work of fiction, and discourages readers from thinking that it is primarily a tract or an editorial. We are urged to ask ourselves: what manner of thing is this book; what kind of fiction is it?

This question has become difficult to ask of *Huckleberry Finn* since Lionel Trilling published, in 1948, his introduction to it in the Rinehart College printing. Trilling praised the book as a nearly perfect work of literature and a work of cardinal significance in American culture. No wonder school principals looked at the book afresh and thought it must be suitable as a text in junior high schools. In the years of the Cold War, the civil rights movement, and protests against the war in Vietnam, it was thought necessary to have some books that held out the possibility of harmony between black people and white; better still, to have books that assured white people that they were already essentially in a right relation to black people and other minorities, even though there might still be local errors and confusions in practice. Within a few years of Trilling's introduction, *Huckleberry*

Finn, as Jonathan Arac has remarked, began to serve "a national and global political function as an icon of integration." It became "a talisman of self-flattering American virtue." Arac maintains that "the importance of this cultural work overrode the offense the book generated among many of its newly authorized, but also newly obligated, African American readers."[34] It seems to me that a reading of the book that stops at the point where it has been deemed to give offence—perhaps because Twain uses the word *nigger* 213 times in it—is inadequate. The book is not a parable. But Trilling bears some responsibility for making it available as a parable. In the scenes on the raft, he tells us, "the boy and the Negro slave form a family, a primitive community—and it is a community of saints."[35] That last phrase is regrettably memorable: neither Huck nor Jim is a saint, unless the word is given a special meaning to accommodate them. Trilling had in view, apparently, such a passage as this one, where Huck and Jim are dividing the watch between them during the storm, while the Duke and the King sleep in the wigwam:

> I had the middle watch, you know, but I was pretty sleepy by that time, so Jim he said he would stand the first half of it for me; he was always mighty good, that way, Jim was. I crawled into the wigwam, but the king and the duke had their legs sprawled around so there warn't no show for me; so I laid outside—I didn't mind the rain, because it was warm, and the waves warn't

> running so high, now. About two they come up again, though, and Jim was going to call me, but he changed his mind because he reckoned they warn't high enough yet to do any harm; but he was mistaken about that, for pretty soon all of a sudden along comes a regular ripper, and washed me overboard. It most killed Jim a-laughing. He was the easiest nigger to laugh that ever was, anyway.
>
> I took the watch, and Jim he laid down and snored away; and by and by the storm let up for good and all; and the first cabin-light that showed, I rousted him out and we slid the raft into hiding-quarters for the day.[36]

Idyllic, yes, and more richly so because we are left to imagine the conversation in which Jim tells Huck that he had thought of waking him up but changed his mind. If only the rest of life could be like that, with laughter and consideration. Trilling seems to have celebrated the book for such perfection of possibility. Admittedly, he expressed a more nuanced sense of the book when he distinguished between the truth of *Tom Sawyer* and that of *Huckleberry Finn:* it is the difference between "truth of honesty" and "a more intense truth, fiercer and more complex."[37] I take this as the distinction between sincerity and authenticity, in Trilling's later terms. In any case, it was unwise of school authorities to nominate *Huckleberry Finn* as required reading. It was equally foolish of other authorities to ban it. In no other English-speaking country but the United States would the book be given such peremptory status.

There is better reason for reading *Huckleberry Finn* as pastoral. In 1935 William Empson published *Some Versions of Pastoral*—the American title is *English Pastoral Poetry*—in which he studied various works of literature and drama to examine "the ways in which the pastoral process of putting the complex into the simple (in itself a great help to the concentration needed for poetry) and the resulting social ideas have been used in English literature." It is a study of rich and poor, peasant and aristocrat, servant and master, the country and the city (though not quite in Raymond Williams's terms), and also a study of the counterrevolutionary claim that "life is essentially inadequate to the human spirit, and yet that a good life must avoid saying so." In pastoral, Empson says, "you take a limited life and pretend it is the full and normal one, and a suggestion that one must do this with all life, because the normal is itself limited, is easily put into the trick though not necessary to its power." This makes possible "a proper or beautiful relation between rich and poor." Or a semblance of such a thing. Empson does not hold that this relation is the social truth of things, or even that it should be: he shows what the convention is doing, and leaves us to decide for or against the sense of life it implies. But he emphasizes at every point the conflicts and tensions that the convention strives to hold at bay. That is why Empson's versions of pastoral are especially sensitive to the forces that make the achievement of social felicity most difficult. Moving the issue to America, pastoral would imagine a tense relation between democracy and some rival value just as attractive in the author's mind. Empson refers at one point to the shift of sentiment "from fool to rogue to child," and his chapter on the Alice books is inspiring on that change.[38] To read *Huckleberry Finn* again in Empson's context would not lead to nostalgia for the bad old good old days when slaves were slaves and people knew their places. But it would remove the simplicities of Cold War rhetoric and its current aftermath.

Afterword

"The true business of literature, as of all intellect, critical or creative, is to remind the powers that be, simple and corrupt as they are, of the turbulence they have to control." I assume that Blackmur meant by that formulation the true social or public business of literature, without prejudice to its private and personal bearing for one reader or another. He added, as a footnote to the turbulence: "There is a disorder vital to the individual which is fatal to society."[1] Presumably he meant that disorder is vital to the individual, else the order he or she maintains is a mere formula, a habit, a device to postpone thinking or make it unnecessary. The classic American books I have been reading have their social value, added to other kinds of value, to the degree to which they clarify for their political masters a new stage in American culture before the Civil War and, in the case of *Huckleberry Finn,* after it. The fact that these books together did not prevent the war, mitigate its virulence, or enlighten the years of Reconstruction is not to be held to their account: intelligence is never enough to instruct the powers that be or to convert vulgar energy, momentum, and turbulence into mind. But if there is a disorder in the culture, it is likely to show itself not only as turbulence at large but as a failure of the individual imagination, at least in some of its respects.

So in another context, Blackmur—whom I quote again without apology—distinguished between three modes of the imagination, two of them adequate to their tasks, the third a sign of disorder within and without. The first two are the narrative imagination and the dramatic imagination, which I take to be, respectively, the faculty of finding order in things to be told, and that of finding order in things to be shown. The third kind is what Blackmur called the symbolic imagination, an unfortunate phrase if only because in next to no time Kenneth Burke, Allen Tate, and other critics were using the same phrase to refer to the supreme reach of the rational imagination, with no defect in sight or in practice. Blackmur deemed it a fault of American literature that it so steadily uses the symbolic imagination rather than the narrative or the dramatic:

> The forest of symbols in [the literature] regards us with a frightening familiarity of glance and we see at once we must find out what those symbols mean or would mean if we could put them together. We see the problematic

> quicker than we see the immediate, and indeed the immediate seems often to have been left out or to have become hidden in remote motions of the imagination. Action is just over the edge of vision, and its symbols draw us on. To D. H. Lawrence, and to other foreign writers, symbolism seemed inherent in the American literary character, or if not inherent seemed the result of an effort to make up for a defect in our culture.[2]

The defect in the culture seems to be penury in the terms available to apprehend it, socially and politically, so that we live not in "an old chaos of the sun"—as Stevens writes—but in the more pressing chaos, opacity and disorder day by day. Blackmur seems to be complaining, in that passage, that American literature doesn't let us see any particular tree in the forest, and scares us with a frightful assertion of meaningfulness while withholding any specific or immediate meaning. Either the meaning is not yet, as in much of Hawthorne's fiction, or is such that no present telling could be enough, as in Melville's *Pierre* and the lurid parts of *Moby-Dick.* "He had no grasp of the particular," Blackmur says of Poe.[3] But Blackmur does not consider whether the symbolic imagination, deemed to be defective and at the service of defect, testifies to a fault in the culture or to an "imp of the perverse" in the writers, such as Poe describes in "The Black Cat":

> And then came, as if to my final and irrevocable overthrow, the spirit of PERVERSENESS. Of this spirit

> philosophy takes no account. Yet I am not more sure that my soul lives, than I am that perverseness is one of the primitive impulses of the human heart—one of the indivisible primary faculties, or sentiments, which give direction to the character of Man. Who has not, a hundred times, found himself committing a vile or a silly action, for no other reason than because he knows he should *not*. Have we not a perpetual inclination, in the teeth of our best judgment, to violate that which is *Law*, merely because we understand it to be such?[4]

The issue as Blackmur puts it becomes clear in the end, but the use of the word *symbolic* confounds it in the process. So much so that I take the first opportunity of getting rid of the word in that use, while holding fast to the issue and the complaint. Guy Davenport is my means.

Davenport has a prejudice just as vigorous as Blackmur's against the forest of symbols, but he cuts a path through it differently. He acknowledges that such forests are raised with the diverse authority of Carlyle, Nerval, Mallarmé, and I would add of Arthur Symons and the early Yeats; so the defect in American culture is not in that culture alone, though it may be a defect greater in degree than the corresponding defect in Europe. The pervasive motives in such a forest, I would say, are revulsion against reality as it is defined in the general culture, and consequently a needy escape into the voluptuousness of dreams and other fictions. The mind of a symbolist either rejects the world and yearns to be shut of it or it otherwise disengages the mind from worldly importunity. Symons expresses the first motive when he writes approvingly of "a literature in which the visible world is no longer a reality, and the unseen world no longer a dream."[5] Yeats expresses the second when he writes that "the purpose of rhythm, it has always seemed to me, is to prolong the moment of contemplation, the moment when we are both asleep and awake, which is the one moment of creation, by hushing us with an alluring monotony, while it holds us waking by variety, to keep us in that state of perhaps real trance, in which the mind liberated from the pressure of the will is unfolded in symbols."[6]

It is not surprising that Davenport gives a severe account of these devices. He is an Objectivist on principle and thinks that "the artist shows the world as if meaning were inherent in its particulars." He has no intention of exchanging particulars for essences or opacities:

> The symbols of the French *symbolistes* and their school from Oslo to Salerno, from Dublin to Budapest, were not properly symbols at all, but enigmas derived from the German doctrine of elective affinities among things and from Fourier and Swedenborg. These symbols so-called in the sensibilities of Baudelaire and Mallarmé became an abstract art, paralleling the disappearance of intelligible images in the painting of Malevich and

> Kandinsky a generation later. You cannot interpret a *symboliste* symbol, you can only contemplate it, like a transcendentalist brooding on the word *nature.*

Not that Davenport is willing to give up symbols, but he wants to change their character and redeem them for use in a better tradition by making them intelligible. He wants a symbol to be such that he can interpret it, come to the end of it, and know what he has come to the end of. He finds authority for this redemption in Pound, Joyce, Zukofsky, other Objectivists, and Eudora Welty. But mainly in Joyce:

> For the first time since Dante, symbols became transparent on Joyce's pages. . . . Joyce, who rethought everything, rethought symbolism. It must first of all be organic, not arbitrary or fanciful. It must be logical, resonant, transparent, bright. From Flaubert he had learned that a true symbol must be found in an image that belongs to the narrative. The parrot Loulou in *Un Coeur simple* acts symbolically to make us feel the devotion, loneliness, ecstasy, and inviolable simplicity of Felicité. . . . In Joyce a rolled-up newspaper with the words *Gold Cup* and *Sceptre* among its racing news becomes a symbolic blossom around which two men, symbolic bees, forage. . . . Joyce's symbols are labyrinths of meaning, but they are logical, and they expand meaning.

> They are, as mediaeval grammarians said, *involucra*—seed husks asking to be peeled.[7]

Blackmur's complaint, translated into these terms, would be that American literature, lacking the social order correspondent to a rational imagination, has resorted to abstractions and enigmas—the white whale, the river, Nature, the scarlet letter, genius—occluded the intelligible image, and paid the price of doing so. It has not had enough vehicles of meaning, so it has had to do all the work—and do it therefore portentously—for itself:

> America has reached—indeed had reached it long ago—a stage of imagination singularly lacking in training in the unconscious skills which afford immediate body to the works of our cultures; less is present by nature in our words, therefore we must put more into them. The immense sophistication of the best American writing—Poe, Hawthorne, James, Melville, and Whitman (who wrote for the most sophisticated possible of audiences, the elite of sophisticated barbarians) was the effect of the need to put more into our words—in short, to invest them as symbols—than came with them at voting age. This is the live heart of Henry James's complaint on behalf of Hawthorne about the American lack of court and church and the various other external costumes of society.[8]

Blackmur might have reminded his readers of Mark Twain's half-serious comment, in *Life on the Mississippi,* about the South—I extend it a little—that when southern gentlemen felt themselves lacking heroic and glamorous images to keep themselves exalted, they took them from Sir Walter Scott: hence Scott was a cause of the Civil War. The first sign of lack in the Emersonian culture of the North was the arduousness with which it got anything done, anything written. No American writer could take life or writing easily, as we see by comparing *Pride and Prejudice* with any American novel written around the same time. Jane Austen seems not to have had to do all the work by herself: much of her meaning (short of her tone of voice) was already there in the social institutions, and had only to be referred to. So her unconscious skills were in easy communion with her conscious skills of irony and tone.

Matthiessen's reading of the American classics is more full-throated than Blackmur's, but it issues in a claim that seems to me doubtful at best. He refers to the literature and "its voicing of fresh aspirations for the rise of the common man." "The one common denominator" he finds in Emerson, Hawthorne, Melville, Thoreau, and Whitman "was their devotion to the possibility of democracy":

> They felt that it was incumbent upon their generation to give fulfillment to the potentialities freed by the Revolution, to provide a culture commensurate with America's political opportunity. Their tones were sometimes opti-

> mistic, sometimes blatantly, even dangerously expansive, sometimes disillusioned, even despairing, but what emerges from the total pattern of their achievement—if we will make the effort to repossess it—is literature for our democracy.

At the end of *American Renaissance,* and with an implication that it is appropriately his last word after six hundred and more pages, Matthiessen quotes Whitman's claim: "I have imagined a life which should be that of the average man in average circumstances, and still grand, heroic."[9]

But in fact none of these writers committed himself to the average man in his average circumstances. Emerson pretended, in "The American Scholar," that he celebrated the rise of the common man. Thoreau didn't bother to conceal his indifference toward such a figure. If you compare Emerson with Dickens and Lawrence in this respect, you see what a genuine interest in ordinary men comes to; though even in the novels of Dickens and Lawrence, ordinary men become distinctive mainly because of the attention the novelists pay to them. In Emerson and Thoreau they are mere abstractions. Emerson and Thoreau were excited only by the vision of an individual's charisma, his (or, more rarely, her) extraordinary magnetism of being. Charisma, in a man or a woman, is what a storm or a flood or a bolt of lightning is at large, a rush of being, exempt from judgment. The perfectibility of man was to be found in great men, not in good or average men. So the classic books do not offer any resistance to the determination of American culture to go for power, conquest, the empire of globalization—the new version of slavery—and if that doesn't make every knee bend, there are always the bombs, nuclear if necessary. If you have dropped them on Hiroshima, why not again somewhere else? In the final sentence of *American Renaissance* Matthiessen claimed that Melville "fulfilled what Coleridge held to be the major function of the artist: he brought 'the whole soul of man into activity.'"[10] It is endearing, but it is not true. There were many aspects of the whole soul of man that Melville did not bring into activity: they had to wait for *The Education of Henry Adams, Mont Saint-Michel and Chartres, The Europeans, The Portrait of a Lady,* "The Bench of Desolation," *The Awkward Age, What Maisie Knew, The Wings of the Dove, The Golden Bowl, The Souls of Black Folk, Black Reconstruction in America, The Fathers, Mary Chesnut's Civil War,* and many (well, at least a few) other works to achieve that aim. Some of these works have—it is their most impressive quality—the misgiving that should modify their certitude. The American classics have little of that misgiving: that is why they are arduous and, like *Walden,* often seem dazzling consistent with their being pert. So it is a pleasure to think that some of these writers might have envisaged a different life, a life in a different relation to power or beauty or silence. I recall Borges's poem "Emerson," in which the poet imagines Emerson closing a volume of Montaigne and going out for a walk in the evening air.

He walks toward the setting sun and reflects on his work, his reading—"I have read the essential books"—his reputation, everything he knows. His next thought is: "No he vivido. Quisiera ser otro hombre"—"I have not lived. I want to be someone else."[11] I wonder who he wanted to be: Montaigne, I imagine. He hardly wanted to be Thoreau or Hawthorne. Such as he was, he is everywhere in American literature: he is, with Thoreau, in Alice Walker's narcissistic *Now Is the Time to Open Your Heart,* and he is also where he mostly—not always—took pride and pleasure in being, in *Leaves of Grass.*

Notes

Introduction: After Emerson

1. T. S. Eliot, "What Is a Classic?" in *On Poetry and Poets* (New York: Farrar, Straus and Cudahy, 1957), pp. 69–70.
2. Ibid., p. 69.
3. Cf. Slavoj Zizek, Preface: "Burning the Bridges," in *The Zizek Reader,* edited by Elizabeth Wright and Edmond Wright (Oxford: Basil Blackwell, 1999), p. vii.
4. Slavoj Zizek, *Welcome to the Desert of the Real* (London: Verso, 2002), p. 80.
5. Frank Kermode, *The Classic* (London: Faber and Faber, 1975), p. 134.
6. Helen Vendler, *Soul Says: On Recent Poetry* (Cambridge: Belknap Press of Harvard University Press, 1995), p. 7.
7. Ezra Pound, *Impact: Essays on Ignorance and the Decline of American Civilization,* edited by Noel Stock (Chicago: Henry Regnery, 1960), pp. 167–168.
8. William Carlos Williams, *In the American Grain* (New York: New Directions, 1956 reprint), p. v.
9. Ibid., p. 65.

10. William Carlos Williams, *Selected Essays* (New York: Random House, 1954), p. 155.
11. R. P. Blackmur, *Language as Gesture: Essays in Poetry* (New York: Harcourt, Brace, 1952), pp. 362–363.
12. *Reading at Risk: A Survey of Literary Reading in America* (National Endowment for the Arts, 2004), p. xi.

1. Emerson and "The American Scholar"

Epigraph: Paul Ricoeur, "Toward a Hermeneutic of the Idea of Revelation," translated by David Pellauer, *Harvard Theological Review,* vol. 70, nos. 1–2 (January–April 1977), p. 30.

1. Henry James, *Partial Portraits* (Ann Arbor: University of Michigan Press, 1970 reprint), p. 6.
2. Ralph Waldo Emerson,"The American Scholar," in *Ralph Waldo Emerson,* The Oxford Authors, edited by Richard Poirier (Oxford: Oxford University Press, 1990), pp. 37, 46.
3. Ibid., p. 38.
4. James, *Partial Portraits,* p. 20.
5. Stanley Cavell, *Emerson's Transcendental Etudes,* edited by David Justin Hodge (Stanford: Stanford University Press, 2003), p. 145.
6. Wallace Stevens, *Collected Poems* (New York: Vintage, 1982), pp. 387, 383.
7. Emerson, "The Transcendentalist," in *Ralph Waldo Emerson,* pp. 101–102.
8. Emerson, "American Scholar," p. 43.
9. Ibid., pp. 37–38.
10. Ibid., p. 39.
11. T. S. Eliot, *On Poetry and Poets* (New York: Farrar, Straus and Cudahy, 1957), p. 72.
12. Ralph Waldo Emerson, "History," in *Early Lectures,* edited by Stephen E. Whicher, Robert E. Spiller, and Wallace E. Williams (Cambridge: Harvard University Press, 3 volumes, 1959–1972), vol. 2, pp. 13, 20. Quoted in Robert D. Richardson Jr., *Emerson: The Mind on Fire* (Berkeley: University of California Press, 1995) pp. 257–258.

13. Emerson, "American Scholar," pp. 40, 41–42.
14. Stevens, *Collected Poems,* p. 524.
15. Emerson, "American Scholar," p. 41.
16. Ibid., p. 43.
17. Ibid., pp. 46, 40–41.
18. Ibid., pp. 50, 51.
19. Cavell, *Emerson's Transcendental Etudes,* p. 160.
20. Stanley Cavell, *Conditions Handsome and Unhandsome: The Constitution of Emersonian Perfectionism* (Chicago: University of Chicago Press, 1990), p. 11.
21. Ralph Waldo Emerson, "Uses of Great Men," *Representative Men,* in *Essays and Lectures* (New York: Library of America, 1983), p. 615.
22. Emerson, "Self-Reliance," in *Ralph Waldo Emerson,* p. 131.
23. Alexis de Toqueville, *Democracy in America,* edited by J. P. Mayer, translated by George Lawrence (New York: Anchor Books, 1969), p. 290.
24. John Dewey, *Individualism Old and New* (New York: Minton, Balch, 1930), p. 14.
25. Charles Taylor, *Sources of the Self: The Making of the Modern Identity* (Cambridge: Harvard University Press, 1989), pp. 131, 132.
26. Emmanuel Levinas, *Totality and Infinity,* translated by Alphonso Lingis (Pittsburgh: Duquesne University Press, 1969), pp. 58, 55.
27. Emmanuel Levinas, *Nine Talmudic Readings,* translated by Annette Aronowicz (Bloomington: Indiana University Press, 1990), p. 99.
28. John Jay Chapman, *Emerson and Other Essays* (1899; New York: AMS Press, second printing, 1969), p. 83.
29. Cited in Cavell, *Emerson's Transcendental Etudes,* pp. 184–185.
30. Chapman, *Emerson and Other Essays,* pp. 106–107.
31. Emerson, "Self-Reliance," p. 133.
32. Cavell, *Emerson's Transcendental Etudes,* p. 8.
33. Ibid., pp. 181, 157.
34. Stanley Cavell, *Conditions Handsome and Unhandsome: The Constitution of Emersonian Perfectionism* (Chicago: University of Chicago Press, 1990), p. 29.
35. Emerson, "American Scholar," p. 46.

36. Hilary Putnam, "Language and Reality," in *Mind, Language, and Reality: Philosophical Papers,* vol. 2 (Cambridge: Cambridge University Press, 1975), p. 272. Putnam quotes Charles Sanders Peirce, *Collected Papers* (Cambridge, Mass., 1958), vol. 5, paragraph 9.
37. Cavell, *Emerson's Transcendental Etudes,* pp. 7, 9.
38. Geoffrey Hill, *Style and Faith* (New York: Counterpoint, 2003), p. 90.
39. Lawrence Sargent Hall: "The Ledge," in *The Best Short Stories of the Modern Age,* edited by Douglas Angus (New York: Fawcett, 1993 reprint), pp. 306, 319, 313.

2. *Moby-Dick*

Epigraph: Robert Lowell, *Collected Poems,* edited by Frank Bidart and David Gewanter (New York: Farrar, Straus and Giroux, 2003), p. 15.

1. Yvor Winters, *In Defense of Reason* (Chicago: Swallow, third edition, 1947), p. 211.
2. Herman Melville, *Moby-Dick; or The Whale,* edited by Harrison Hayford, Hershel Parker, and G. Thomas Tanselle (Evanston: Northwestern University Press and Newberry Library, 1988), pp. 327–328.
3. C. L. R. James, *Mariners, Renegades, and Castaways: The Story of Herman Melville and the World We Live In* (New York: C. L. R. James, 1953), p. 62.
4. Melville, *Moby-Dick.*, pp. 198, 202.
5. James, *Mariners, Renegades, and Castaways,* p. 14.
6. Perry Miller, *Nature's Nation* (Cambridge: Belknap Press of Harvard University Press, 1967) pp. 255, 256.
7. F. O. Matthiessen, *American Renaissance: Art and Expression in the Age of Emerson and Whitman* (London: Oxford University Press, 1941; fourth impression 1949), pp. 457, 459.
8. F. O. Matthiessen, *From the Heart of Europe* (New York: Oxford University Press, 1948), p. 37.
9. Marius Bewley, *The Eccentric Design: Form in the Classic American Novel* (New York: Columbia University Press, 1959), pp. 205, 206, 208, 214.

10. Donald E. Pease, *Visionary Compacts: American Renaissance Writings in Cultural Context* (Madison, Wisconsin: University of Wisconsin Press, 1987) pp. 243–245, 274, 270, 271.
11. E. M. Cioran, *The Temptation to Exist,* translated by Richard Howard (Chicago: Quadrangle, 1968), pp. 126, 127.
12. James Guetti, *Word-Music: The Aesthetic Aspect of Narrative Fiction* (New Brunswick: Rutgers University Press, 1980), p. 100.
13. Donald Pease, "C. L. R. James, *Moby-Dick,* and the Emergence of Transnational American Studies," *Arizona Quarterly,* vol. 56, no. 3 (Autumn 2000), pp. 109–110.
14. Donald Davie, *Two Ways Out of Whitman* (Manchester: Carcanet, 2000), p. 25.
15. R. P. Blackmur, "Introduction to *American Short Stories,*" in *Outsider at the Heart of Things: Essays by R. P. Blackmur,* edited by James T. Jones (Urbana: University of Illinois Press, 1989), p. 195.
16. R. P. Blackmur, *The Lion and the Honeycomb: Essays in Solicitude and Critique* (New York: Harcourt, Brace, 1955), p. 131.
17. Pease, *Visionary Compacts,* p. 37.
18. Winters, *In Defense of Reason,* pp. 209, 211, 213.
19. Northrop Frye, *A World in a Grain of Sand,* edited by Robert D. Denham (New York: Peter Lang, 1991), p. 123.
20. James, *Mariners, Renegades, and Castaways,* p. 5.
21. Denis Donoghue, *Thieves of Fire* (London: Faber and Faber, 1973), p. 94.
22. Robert Martin Adams, *Nil: Episodes in the Literary Conquest of Void During the Nineteenth Century* (New York: Oxford University Press, 1966), p. 143.
23. James Guetti, *The Limits of Metaphor: A Study of Melville, Conrad, and Faulkner* (Ithaca: Cornell University Press, 1967), pp. 157–159.
24. F. R. Leavis, *The Great Tradition* (Garden City: Doubleday, 1954) p. 219.
25. Adams, *Nil,* p. 146.
26. Carl Schmitt, *Der Begriff des Politichen* (1932), translated by George Schwab as *The Concept of the Political* (New Brunswick: Rutgers University Press, 1976), pp. 28–30. Quoted in Jacques Derrida, *Politics of Friendship,* translated by George Collins (London: Verso, 1997), p. 88.

27. Jacques Derrida: "Le siècle et le pardon," interview with Michel Wieviorka, *Le Monde des debats,* December 1999, pp. 10–17.
28. Melville, *Moby-Dick,* p. 522.
29. Charles Olson, *Call Me Ishmael* (New York: Reynal and Hitchcock, 1947), p. 73.
30. Yvor Winters, *In Defense of Reason,* p. 201.
31. James Wood, *The Broken Estate: Essays on Literature and Belief* (London: Jonathan Cape, 1999), p. 33.
32. Donoghue, *Thieves of Fire,* p. 94.
33. Northrop Frye, *Anatomy of Criticism* (Princeton: Princeton University Press, 1990 reprint), p. 92.
34. Ibid., p. 313.
35. Kenneth Burke, *A Grammar of Motives and A Rhetoric of Motives* (Cleveland: World, 1962), pp. 406–407.
36. Michel de Certeau, *The Practice of Everyday Life,* translated by Steven Rendall (Berkeley: University of California Press, 1988 reprint), p. xviii.
37. Herbert G. Eldridge: "'Careful Disorder': The Structure of *Moby-Dick*": *American Literature,* vol. 34, no. 2 (May 1967), pp. 146, 151.
38. Melville, *Moby-Dick,* p. 289.
39. Blackmur, *Lion and the Honeycomb,* pp. 124–125.
40. William V. Spanos, *The Errant Art of Moby-Dick: The Canon, the Cold War, and the Struggle for American Studies* (Durham: Duke University Press, 1995), pp. 124, 128, 167.
41. Ibid., p. 60.
42. Herman Melville, *Pierre; or, The Ambiguities,* edited by Harrison Hayford, Herschel Parker, and G. Thomas Tanselle (Evanston: Northwestern University Press and Newberry Library, 1971), p. 141.
43. Melville, *Moby-Dick,* p. 361.
44. Spanos, *Errant Art of Moby-Dick,* p. 86.
45. Melville, *Moby-Dick,* pp. 346–347.
46. Ibid., pp. 424–425.

3. *The Scarlet Letter*

Epigraph: Robert Lowell, *Collected Poems,* edited by Frank Bidart and David Gewanter (New York: Farrar, Straus and Giroux, 2003), p. 352.

1. Bernard J. Kelly, *Apologetics and Catholic Doctrine,* part 3, *Catholic Doctrine* (Dublin: Gill, third impression, 1954), pp. 25, 26.
2. James Joyce, *A Portrait of the Artist as a Young Man,* edited by Hans Walter Gabler with Walter Hettche (New York: Garland, 1993), p. 188.
3. Graham Greene, *The Heart of the Matter* (New York: Penguin, 1999 reprint), pp. 186–187, 206.
4. Nathaniel Hawthorne, *The French and Italian Notebooks,* edited by Thomas Woodson (Columbus: Ohio State University Press, 1980), p. 215.
5. Nathaniel Hawthorne, *The Scarlet Letter,* edited by Sculley Bradley, Richmond Croom Beatty, E. Hudson Long, and Seymour Gross (New York: W. W. Norton, second edition, 1978), pp. 144–146.
6. Ibid., pp. 140, 41, 51.
7. Nathaniel Hawthorne, "Earth's Holocaust," in *Tales and Sketches* (New York: Library of America, 1982), p. 906.
8. Thomas Hooker, "A True Sight of Sin," in *The American Puritans: Their Prose and Poetry,* edited by Perry Miller (New York: Columbia University Press, 1956), p. 156.
9. Hawthorne, *Scarlet Letter,* p. 182.
10. William Empson, *Argufying: Essays on Literature and Culture,* edited by John Haffenden (Iowa City: University of Iowa Press, 1987), p. 473.
11. Hawthorne, "The Minister's Black Veil," in *Tales and Sketches,* pp. 373, 383–384.
12. Hawthorne, *Scarlet Letter,* p. 140.
13. Hawthorne, "Minister's Black Veil," p. 381.
14. Empson, *Argufying,* p. 474.
15. Hawthorne, *The Marble Faun; or, The Romance of Monte Beni* (Columbus: Ohio State University Press, 1968), p. 359.
16. Hawthorne, *Scarlet Letter,* p. 154.
17. Hawthorne, *Marble Faun,* p. 94.

18. Hawthorne, *Scarlet Letter,* p. 126.
19. Henry James, *Literary Criticism,* vol. 1, *Essays on Literature, American Writers, English Writers* (New York: Library of America,1984), pp. 325–326, 362, 363, 365, 396, 368, 366.
20. Q. D. Leavis, "Hawthorne as Poet," *Collected Essays,* edited by G. Singh (Cambridge: Cambridge University Press, 1985). vol. 2, p. 45.
21. Hawthorne, "Main Street," in *Tales and Sketches,* p. 1038–1039.
22. Allen Tate, "Emily Dickinson," in *Essays of Four Decades* (Chicago: Swallow, 1968), pp. 283, 294.
23. R. P. Blackmur, "Emily Dickinson," in *Selected Essays,* edited by Denis Donoghue (New York: Ecco, 1986), pp. 178, 195, 179.
24. Tate, "Emily Dickinson," p. 285.
25. Ralph Waldo Emerson, "Experience," in *Selected Writings,* edited by Brooks Atkinson (New York: Modern Library, 1950), pp. 360–361.
26. Emerson, "Experience," ibid., p. 284.
27. R. P. Blackmur, "Afterword to Hawthorne's Tales," in *Outsider at the Heart of Things: Essays by R. P. Blackmur,* edited by James T. Jones (Urbana: University of Illinois Press, 1989), p. 272.
28. Tate, *Essays of Four Decades,* p. 287.
29. Ibid.
30. Wallace Stevens, "Sunday Morning," in *The Palm at the End of the Mind,* edited by Holly Stevens (New York: Vintage, 1990), p. 8.
31. G. W. F. Hegel, *Phenomenology of Spirit,* translated by A. V. Miller (Oxford: Oxford University Press, 1977), p. 5.
32. T. S. Eliot, Introduction to Djuna Barnes, *Nightwood* (New York: Harcourt, Brace, 1937), pp. xii–xiii.
33. Hawthorne, "Dr. Bullivant," in *Tales and Sketches,* pp. 34–35.
34. Hawthorne, "The May-Pole of Merry Mount," ibid., pp. 362, 366.
35. Blackmur, "Afterword to Hawthorne's Tales," p. 268.
36. Hawthorne, "Egotism; or, The Bosom Serpent," in *Tales and Sketches,* pp. 793, 785.

37. Quoted in William Ramp: "Effervescence, Differentiation and Representation in *The Elementary Forms,*" in *On Durkheim's Elementary Forms of Religious Life,* edited by N. J. Allen, W. S. F. Pickering, and W. Watts Miller (New York: Routledge, 1998), p. 145.
38. Blackmur, "Afterword to Hawthorne's Tales," p. 272–273. Cf. Leo Spitzer, "Speech and Language in *Inferno* XIII," in *Representative Essays,* edited by Alban K. Forcione, Herbert Lindenberger, and Madeline Sutherland (Stanford: Stanford University Press, 1988), pp. 148–149: "There is a great gulf between the belief of a Dante in the objective reality of expiation (even though the nature of the manifold punishments be shaped by his imagination) and the almost whimsical attitude of a Hawthorne, who writes romantic novels of expiation. The representations of this novelist (who was acquainted with the punishment-by-*contrappasso* of both Bunyan and Dante) are tempered with an 'as if,' or an 'as it were': he raises questions that invite new possibilities of interpretation, he introduces suggestions meant to anticipate the 'smile' of the sophisticated modern reader. There is not with him the firmness of design that characterizes the work of Dante; whereas the medieval poet affirms unhesitatingly always the *one* inevitable consequence of a sin, Hawthorne seems willfully to attenuate the very correspondence he has established between sin and punishment, offering this as something fortuitous, as something which might have been otherwise: he is an heir to the tradition of deep-rooted belief, but he makes of this a folkloristic quicksand."
39. Blackmur, "Afterword to Hawthorne's Tales," p. 273.
40. Emily Brontë, *Wuthering Heights,* edited by Ian Jack (Oxford: Oxford University Press, 1995), pp. 80–82.
41. Frank Kermode, *The Classic* (London: Faber and Faber, 1975), pp. 104–105.
42. Empson, *Argufying,* p. 474.
43. Jorge Luis Borges, *Other Inquisitions, 1937–1952,* translated by Ruth L. C. Simms (Austin: University of Texas Press, 2000 reprint), p. 56–57.

4. *Walden*

1. Ralph Waldo Emerson, "Thoreau," in *Selected Writings,* edited by Brooks Atkinson (New York: Modern Library, 1950), pp. 910, 898.
2. Kathleen Modenbach, "Revisiting Walden Pond in 2003," *Education World,* http://www.education-world.com/a_curr/profdev063.shtml.
3. John P. Diggins, "Thoreau, Marx, and the 'Riddle' of Alienation," *Social Research,* vol. 39, no. 4 (Winter 1972), p. 571.
4. Lionel Trilling, "Freud: Within and Beyond Culture," in *Beyond Culture: Essays on Literature and Learning* (New York: Harcourt Brace Jovanovich, 1978), p. 93.
5. Trilling, "On the Teaching of Modern Literature," ibid., pp. 26–27.
6. Cf. Joseph Dunne, "Beyond Sovereignty and Deconstruction: The Storied Self," *Philosophy and Social Criticism,* vol. 21, nos. 5–6 (September–November 1995), p. 140.
7. Trilling, "On the Teaching of Modern Literature," p. 27.
8. Robert Hughes, "Winslow Homer," in *Nothing If Not Critical: Selected Essays on Art and Artists* (London: Harvill, 1990), p. 107.
9. Lawrence Buell, *The Environmental Imagination: Thoreau, Nature Writing, and the Formation of American Culture* (Cambridge: Belknap Press of Harvard University Press, 1995), pp. 32, 171.
10. Sharon Cameron, *Writing Nature: Henry Thoreau's Journal* (New York: Oxford University Press, 1985), pp. 30, 46.
11. Leo Marx, "The Full Thoreau," *New York Review of Books,* vol. 46, no. 12 (July 15, 1999).
12. Leo Marx, "An Exchange on Thoreau," *New York Review of Books,* vol. 46, no. 19 (December 2, 1999).
13. William Empson, *Some Versions of Pastoral* (New York: New Directions, fifth printing, 1974), p. 11.
14. Ibid., p. 4.
15. Emerson, "Thoreau," p. 897.
16. Jean Starobinski, "The Style of Autobiography," in *Literary Style: A Symposium,* edited by Seymour Chatman (New York: Oxford University Press, 1971), p. 288.

17. Henry David Thoreau, *Walden, or Life in the Woods,* in *A Week on the Concord and Merrimack Rivers; Walden, or Life in the Woods; The Maine Woods; Cape Cod* (New York: Library of America, 1985), pp. 400–401.
18. Northrop Frye, *Anatomy of Criticism: Four Essays* (Princeton: Princeton University Press, tenth printing 1990), p. 310.
19. Thoreau, *Walden,* pp. 566, 429, 578.
20. Cameron, *Writing Nature,* p. 75.
21. Thoreau, *Walden,* pp. 575–576.
22. Ralph Waldo Emerson, "School," in *The Early Lectures,* edited by Stephen E. Whicher, Robert E. Spiller, and Wallace E. Williams (Cambridge: Harvard University Press, 3 volumes, 1959–1972), vol. 3, p. 49.
23. Thoreau, *Walden,* p. 548.
24. Thoreau, *A Week on the Concord and Merrimack Rivers,* in *A Week on the Concord and Merrimack Rivers* . . . , p. 310.
25. Thoreau, *Walden,* pp. 547, 476.
26. Henry D. Thoreau, *Journal,* vol. 4, *1851–1852,* edited by Leonard N. Neufeldt and Nancy Craig Simmons (Princeton: Princeton University Press, 1992), p. 181.
27. Wallace Stevens, "The Snow Man," *Collected Poems* (New York: Vintage, 1990), pp. 9–10.
28. Empson, *Some Versions of Pastoral,* p. 187.
29. Thoreau, *Journal,* vol. 5, *1852–1853,* edited by Patrick F. O'Connell (Princeton: Princeton University Press, 1997), p. 164 (June 30, 1852).
30. Thoreau, *Cape Cod,* in *A Week on the Concord and Merrimack Rivers* . . . , p. 979.
31. Empson, *Some Versions of Pastoral,* pp. 264–265.
32. Thoreau, *Walden,* pp. 553–554.
33. Ibid., p. 498.
34. Thoreau, *Journal,* vol. 4, p. 176 (November 11, 1851).
35. Thoreau, *Cape Cod,* p. 853.
36. Thoreau, *A Week on the Concord and Merrimack Rivers,* p. 216.
37. Thoreau, *Journal,* vol. 4, p. 435.

38. Henry D. Thoreau, "Life Without Principle," in *Collected Essays and Poems* (New York: Library of America, 2001), p. 365.
39. Thoreau, "Natural History of Massachusetts," ibid., p. 22.
40. Thoreau, *Walden,* pp. 495, 412, 579.
41. Ibid., p. 429.
42. Emerson, "Nature," in *Selected Writings,* p. 4; Emerson, "The American Scholar," ibid., 52.
43. Dunne, "Beyond Sovereignty and Deconstruction," p. 138.
44. Thoreau, *Walden,* p. 363.
45. Thoreau, *A Week on the Concord and Merrimack Rivers,* p. 113.
46. Edward Dahlberg, "Thoreau and *Walden,*" *The Edward Dahlberg Reader,* edited by Paul Carroll (New York: New Directions, 1967), p. 274.
47. Thoreau, *Walden,* pp.559–560.
48. Thoreau, *A Week on the Concord and Merrimack Rivers,* p. 85.
49. Thoreau, *Journal,* vol. 4, p. 178 (November 12, 1851).
50. Thoreau, *Walden,* p. 514.
51. Starobinski, "The Style of Autobiography," p. 74.
52. Emily Brontë, *Wuthering Heights,* edited by David Daiches (Harmondsworth: Penguin, 1985 reprint), p. 367.
53. Thoreau, *Walden,* pp. 395–396.
54. Thoreau, *A Week on the Concord and Merrimack Rivers,* p. 48.

5. *Leaves of Grass*

1. Wallace Stevens, "Like Decorations in a Nigger Cemetery," in *The Collected Poems* (New York: Vintage, 1990), p. 150.
2. Stevens, "The Idea of Order at Key West," ibid., p. 128; Stevens, "The Comedian as the Letter C," ibid., 33; Stevens, "Like Decorations in a Nigger Cemetery," p. 155.
3. Wallace Stevens, *Letters,* edited by Holly Stevens (Berkeley: University of California Press, 1996), pp. 870–871.
4. Walt Whitman, "Democratic Vistas," in *Complete Poetry and Collected Prose* (New York: Library of America, 1982), p. 930.

5. Walt Whitman, Preface to the first (1855) edition of *Leaves of Grass,* in *Leaves of Grass and Other Writings,* edited by Michael Moon (New York: W. W. Norton, 2002), p. 616.
6. F. O. Matthiessen, *American Renaissance: Art and Expression in the Age of Emerson and Whitman* (London: Oxford University Press, fourth impression, 1949), p. 651; Thoreau quoted, p. 649.
7. George Santayana, *Interpretations of Poetry and Religion* (New York: Scribner, 1900), pp. 176–177, 179, 182.
8. R. P. Blackmur, *Anni Mirabiles, 1921–1925: Reason in the Madness of Letters* (Washington, D.C.: Library of Congress, 1956), pp. 33–34.
9. Quentin Anderson, "Whitman's New Man," in Walt Whitman, *Walt Whitman's Autograph Revision of the Analysis of "Leaves of Grass" (for Dr. R. M. Bucke's "Walt Whitman"* (New York: New York University Press, 1974), pp. 45, 46.
10. Yvor Winters, *In Defense of Reason* (Chicago: Swallow, third edition, 1947), pp. 590, 591.
11. Ezra Pound, *The Spirit of Romance* (London, n.d.), p. 163. Quoted in Herbert Bergman, "Ezra Pound and Walt Whitman," *American Literature,* vol. 27, no. 1 (March 1955), p. 56.
12. T. S. Eliot, "The Function of Criticism," *Selected Prose of T. S. Eliot,* edited by Frank Kermode (New York: Harcourt Brace Jovanovich, 1975), p. 73.
13. Cf. Jorge Luis Borges, *Other Inquisitions, 1937–1952,* translated by Ruth L. C. Simms (Austin: University of Texas Press, 1964), p. 68.
14. Hugh Kenner, *The Invisible Poet: T. S. Eliot* (New York: McDowell, Obolensky, 1959), p. 40.
15. Donald Davie, *Articulate Energy: An Inquiry into the Syntax of English Poetry* (London: Routledge and Kegan Paul, 1955), p. 89.
16. W. B. Yeats, "Byzantium," in *The Variorum Edition of the Poems,* edited by Peter Allt and Russell K. Alspach (New York: Macmillan, 1987), p. 497.
17. Allen Grossman, "The Poetics of Union in Whitman and Lincoln: An Inquiry Toward the Relationship of Art and Policy," in *The American Renaissance Reconsidered,* edited by Walter Benn Michaels and Donald E. Pease (Baltimore: Johns Hopkins University Press, 1985), pp. 188–189.

18. Sir Thomas Wyatt, "They Flee from Me That Sometime Did Me Seek," in *Collected Poems,* edited by Kenneth Muir and Patricia Thomson (Liverpool: Liverpool University Press, 1969), p. 27.
19. Rosemund Tuve, *Elizabethan and Metaphysical Imagery,* quoted in Davie, *Articulate Energy,* p. 22.
20. Grossman, "Poetics of Union," pp. 192–194, 199.
21. Whitman, "When Lilacs Last in the Dooryard Bloom'd," in *Leaves of Grass and Other Writings,* p. 278.
22. Grossman, "Poetics of Union," pp. 188–189.
23. Ibid., pp. 188, 192
24. Whitman, "By Blue Ontario's Shore," in *Leaves of Grass and Other Writings,* p. 292.
25. Grossman, "Poetics of Union," pp. 201–202, 203.
26. Whitman, "To You," *Leaves of Grass and Other Writings,* p. 195.
27. William James, *Pragmatism: A New Name for Some Old Ways of Thinking* (New York: Longmans, Green, 1907), pp. 273–301.
28. Whitman, "Of the Terrible Doubt of Appearances," in *Leaves of Grass and Other Writings,* p. 103.
29. Whitman, "Song of Myself," in *Leaves of Grass and Other Writings,* p. 34.
30. John Hollander, *The Figure of Echo: A Mode of Allusion in Milton and After* (Berkeley: University of California Press, 1981), pp. 122–123.
31. Cf. Michael Moon, "The Twenty-Ninth Bather," in Whitman, *Leaves of Grass and Other Writings,* p. 861.
32. Josephine Miles, *Eras and Modes in English Poetry* (Berkeley: University of California Press, 1957), pp. 49, 56–57.
33. Whitman, "Give Me the Splendid Silent Sun," *Leaves of Grass and Other Writings,* p. 263.
34. Gerard Manley Hopkins, "The Leaden Echo and the Golden Echo," in *Poems and Prose,* edited by W. H. Gardner (London: Penguin, 1985 reprint), pp. 52, 54.
35. Whitman, *Leaves of Grass* (1855), *Complete Poetry and Collected Prose,* pp. 29, 30.

36. Ibid., p. 47.
37. Whitman, Preface to 1876 edition of *Leaves of Grass and Two Rivulets,* in *Leaves of Grass and Other Writings,* pp. 658–659.
38. Louis Simpson, "Walt Whitman at Bear Mountain," in *Collected Poems* (New York: Paragon, 1988), pp. 162–163.
39. William H. Gass, *Habitations of the Word* (New York: Simon and Schuster, 1985), p. 17.
40. Ibid., p. 21.

6. *Adventures of Huckleberry Finn*

1. Philip Rahv, *Image and Idea: Fourteen Essays on Literary Themes* (Norfolk, Conn.: New Directions, 1949), pp. 1–2.
2. Leslie A. Fiedler, *Love and Death in the American Novel* (New York: Criterion, 1960), p. 186.
3. Edgar Allan Poe, *Selections from Poe's Literary Criticism,* edited by John Brooks Moore (New York: F. S. Crofts, 1926), p. 136.
4. Marius Bewley, *The Complex Fate: Hawthorne, Henry James, and Some Other American Writers* (London: Chatto and Windus, 1952), pp. 2–3.
5. F. R. Leavis, Introduction, *The Complex Fate,* pp. ix, xi.
6. Marius Bewley, *The Eccentric Design: Form in the Classic American Novel* (New York: Columbia University Press, 1959), p. 290.
7. T. S. Eliot, "American Literature and the American Language," *To Criticize the Critic, and Other Writings* (New York: Farrar, Straus and Giroux, 1965), pp. 54, 53.
8. Bewley, *The Eccentric Design,* p. 292.
9. Bewley, *The Complex Fate,* p. 192.
10. Mark Twain, Notebook entry, in *The Works of Mark Twain,* vol. 8, *Adventures of Huckleberry Finn,* edited by Walter Blair and Victor Fischer (Berkeley: University of California Press, 1988), pp. 806–807.
11. Mark Twain, *Mark Twain's Notebook,* Prepared for Publication with Comments by Albert Bigelow Paine (New York: Harper and Brothers Publishers, 1935) pp. 348–349.

12. Twain, Notebook entry, in *Huckleberry Finn,* p. 806.
13. Mark Twain, *Pudd'nhead Wilson,* edited by Malcolm Bradbury (London: Penguin, 1986 reprint), p. 225.
14. Mark Twain, *The Adventures of Tom Sawyer,* (New York: Penguin, 1986 reprint), pp. 219–220.
15. Leo Marx, *The Pilot and the Passenger: Essays on Literature, Technology, and Culture in the United States* (New York: Oxford University Press, 1988), p. 42.
16. Richard Poirier, *A World Elsewhere: The Place of Style in American Literature* (New York: Oxford University Press, 1966), pp. 179, 189, 15–16.
17. Fiedler, *Love and Death in the American Novel,* pp. 590–591.
18. Twain, *Huckleberry Finn,* pp. 123–124.
19. Ibid., pp. 268–269, 270–271, 362.
20. T. S. Eliot, "The Dry Salvages," in *Collected Poems, 1909–1962* (New York: Harcourt Brace, 1963), p. 191.
21. T. S. Eliot, Introduction to *Huckleberry Finn,* reprinted in *Adventures of Huckleberry Finn,* edited by Thomas Cooley (New York: W. W. Norton, 1999 reprint), p. 353.
22. Eliot, "American Literature and the American Language," p. 54.
23. Eliot, "The Dry Salvages," p. 191.
24. Eliot, Introduction to *Huckleberry Finn,* p. 352.
25. T. S. Eliot, "*Ulysses,* Order, and Myth," *The Dial,* November 1923; reprinted in *Selected Prose of T. S. Eliot,* edited by Frank Kermode (New York: Harcourt Brace Jovanovich, 1975), pp. 177–178.
26. Cf. R. P. Blackmur, *A Primer of Ignorance,* edited by Joseph Frank (New York: Harcourt, Brace, 1967), p. 41.
27. Eliot, *The Waste Land, Collected Poems, 1909–1962,* p. 62.
28. T. S. Eliot, "John Marston," in *Selected Essays* (London: Faber and Faber, 1963), p. 232.
29. Eliot, Introduction to *Huckleberry Finn,* p. 353.
30. Ibid., pp. 349, 350.
31. Leo Marx, *Pilot and the Passenger,* p. 45.

32. Eliot, "The Dry Salvages," p. 191.
33. T. S. Eliot, *The Sacred Wood* (London: Methuen, 1960 reprint), pp. viii–x.
34. Jonathan Arac, *"Huckleberry Finn" as Idol and Target* (Madison: University of Wisconsin Press, 1997), pp. 21, 62.
35. Lionel Trilling, "The Greatness of *Huckleberry Finn*," reprinted in *Adventures of Huckleberry Finn,* edited by Sculley Bradley, Richmond Croom Beatty, E. Hudson Long, and Thomas Cooley (New York: W. W. Norton, 1977), p. 321.
36. Twain, *Huckleberry Finn,* p. 168.
37. Trilling, "The Greatness of *Huckleberry Finn,*" p. 319.
38. William Empson, *Some Versions of Pastoral* (London: Chatto and Windus, second impression, 1950), pp. 23, 114, 196, 259.

Afterword

1. R. P. Blackmur, "The Politics of Human Power," in *The Lion and the Honeycomb: Essays in Solicitude and Critique* (New York: Harcourt, Brace, 1955), p. 41.
2. R. P. Blackmur, "Introduction to *American Short Stories,*" in *Outsider at the Heart of Things: Essays by R. P. Blackmur,* edited by James T. Jones (Urbana: University of Illinois Press, 1989), p. 190.
3. Blackmur, "Afterword to Poe's Tales," ibid., p. 226.
4. Edgar Allen Poe, "The Black Cat," in *Selected Writings,* edited by David Galloway (Baltimore: Penguin, 1967), p. 322. Quoted in Blackmur, "Afterword to Poe's Tales," pp. 229–230.
5. Arthur Symons, *The Symbolist Movement in Literature,* with an introduction by Richard Ellmann (New York: Dutton, 1958), pp. 2–3.
6. W. B. Yeats, "The Symbolism of Poetry," in *Essays and Introductions* (London: Macmillan, 1961), p. 159.
7. Guy Davenport, *The Geography of the Imagination* (San Francisco: North Point, 1981), pp. 262–263.
8. Blackmur, "Introduction to *American Short Stories,*" p. 190.

9. F. O. Matthiessen, *American Renaissance: Art and Expression in the Age of Emerson and Whitman* (London: Oxford University Press, 1941), pp. vii, ix, xv, 650.
10. Ibid., p. 656.
11. Jorge Luis Borges, "Emerson," translated by Mark Strand, *Selected Poems, 1923–1967*, edited by Norman Thomas Di Giovanni (New York: Delacorte/ Seymour Lawrence, 1972), pp. 170–171.

Acknowledgment

I am grateful to the editors of *Law and Literature, The Sewanee Review,* and *Christianity and Literature* for permission to reprint chapters that appeared, in earlier forms, in their journals.

D.D.

Index